X
4

WITHDRAWN

COUNSELING SERVICES
FOR
ADULTS IN HIGHER EDUCATION

edited by
MARTHA L. FARMER

The City College of
The City University of New York

The Scarecrow Press, Inc.
Metuchen, N. J.   1971

378.194
C855
1971

ISBN 0-8108-0443-3

Library of Congress Catalog Card Number 78-167648

"I am a part of all that I have met:
Yet all experience is an arch wherethro'
Gleams the untravell'd world, whose
Margin fades for ever and for ever as I move."

Alfred Lord Tennyson, "Ulysses"

Preface

The present and predicted increase in the number of men and women returning to or entering higher education has made a book such as this a necessity for those concerned with adult counseling services.

The Adult Student Personnel Association, recognizing the need for a reference work in their field, invited a number of professionals in adult counseling to contribute chapters in their specialties. The Association is indebted to these individuals who despite their busy schedules and professional commitments have used their expertise to add to our knowledge of counseling services for adults in higher education.

It is difficult to single out any one individual for his excellent contribution. However, a special word of thanks is due Clarence H. Thompson, Dean of University College, Center for Continuing Education, Drake University, who consented to write the opening chapter while in office as President of the Association of University Evening Colleges.

The authors were also generous in assigning any royalties, derived from the sale of this book, over to the Adult Student Personnel Association, which underwrote the cost of preparing the manuscript for publication. The Association will use these royalties to establish research grants which it hopes will stimulate further investigations into the nature of adult counseling. The royalties will also be used to develop a consulting service which will be available at a minimum or no charge to member institutions depending on their location. Nonmember colleges which wish to broaden or establish counseling services for adults also may use this service for a set fee. It is hoped that, through these endeavors, adult students can have available a truly meaningful counseling service designed for their needs.

The Association is deeply indebted to Phyllis Y. Hird for the time and effort she put into assisting in the editing of the manuscript. Without her invaluable aid, the deadline for publication would not have been met.

Gratitude is also due Phillip L. Garcia, formerly Assistant Dean and Director of Academic Services, Livingston College, Rutgers University, now Deputy Director of the Puerto Rican Convention of New Jersey, for his contribution in indexing this book.

Martha L. Farmer

Contents

INTRODUCTION

When the historian of the future comes to record the ferment and change in American education during the past decade, he will of necessity devote considerable attention to the unique and expanding role of adult higher education in the United States and Canada. In so doing, he will be giving recognition to events of an explosive nature represented in numbers, programs, and services which come within the broad category of adult higher education.

When Martha Farmer, of the City University, asked me to write the introduction for this needed book, I felt privileged and happy for the opportunity. I have long thought that counseling is one of the essential ingredients for successful and meaningful adult higher education programs. I have witnessed during my own professional career not only expanding needs, but also, with satisfaction, the resources becoming available in this field.

It was in 1960 that Martha Farmer, with the encouragement of the late Ralph Kendall, Dean of Adult and Continuing Education in the University of Toledo, made the first serious and scholarly attempt to assess what was needed and what was being done in the field of counseling in evening college and other higher education programs for adults.

The contributions of the various authors herein give evidence of the need for counseling services if college and university adult education programs are to be a significant factor in higher education, and in society as a whole.

We have always had some form of adult education. Adult higher education is a "Johnny-come-lately." The last 30 years have seen the emergence of the evening college as an important instrument of higher education. Before that, there were classes for adults. There have always been "classes."

It was interesting to realize, during one of my trips around New England, that the first adult education classes in Massachusetts probably started on the island of Nantucket when the old whaling captains who had been around the world returned to port. They decided that one of the best things they could do during the long winter evenings would be to teach those on the island who would like to learn the knowledge they had acquired of celestial navigation and astronomy. They offered classes to adults, young and old, in which they might learn to become something more than a deck hand. They could learn how to pilot and steer a ship, and acquire skills necessary to rise to the position of mate or captain. In many regions of Europe, especially in Scandinavia, one finds folk schools which exist to teach adults; adult training programs have historically been a part of England's informal educational system.

Until approximately the year 1938, most colleges and universities, if they were aware of evening schools or adult higher education, never conceived of it as an arm of higher education per se but as a peripheral area. Administrators considered it as an expanding field capable of providing income which, while not academically respectable, was financially enticing. In the literature of the first third of this century, adult education was never expressed in terms that made it a valid form of higher education. All the rationalizations and generalizations contended that there did not exist a body of knowledge distinctly appropriate to teaching adults beyond high school; or, if there were, it was inferior and standards of excellence as are applied to college curricula need not be applied to it.

World War II made the greatest impact in changing this status quo with the advent of Public Law 550, the G.I. Bill. Evening colleges attracted in vast numbers adults who had received various kinds of training in the armed services. In the aftermath of the war, colleges and universities, particularly urban schools of higher learning, found themselves faced with a great problem as to how to cope with so many veterans' educational needs.

This pressure did not arise because of men and women demanding to be admitted into regular daytime college programs. A great many were married, had procured jobs, and had started the creation of their home and family and yet realized that they lived in a competitive world which was vastly and quickly changing. It is difficult to appreciate how fast this change took place. We accept the fact of change and yet are not always conscious that we are living through and within it.

x

Universities and colleges with evening programs, particularly those in urban areas, began to experience this influx of students. They began to develop programs which could lead to a baccalaureate degree. This was the first step. The handicap the adult student and the institution faced, not fully overcome even today (but which existed in very sharp image in those days), was that adult higher education wherever and whenever it was available was considered to be marginal and less than respectable. It was endured by college faculties who felt that there was little they could do to stem the tide other than to make sure that it did not interfere with regular day programs or encroach on facilities and privileges. Administrators endured it because they assumed they could take the criticism of those who might not understand it, as it provided use of existing facilities that would generate income with which to build new buildings and help to provide funds for growth. It is not naive to observe that the cost of running adult programs provides funds that do not have to be allocated to the support of ancillary enterprises like athletics and student activities associated with campus living.

This growth of adult higher education and counseling services did not have universal acceptance. There were many who felt it was not intellectually viable. One must objectively point out that there was some justification for this point of view. In too many cases, programs were established without critical examination of fundamental criteria.

There existed no consensus or even general agreement as to what constituted adult higher education nor was there any feeling that adult experience could be translated into, or measured in terms of education. It was only when Brooklyn College made its experiment in evaluating adult experience in the liberal arts that ability to recognize elements of adult educational mensuration, and the need for adult counseling services, were given tangible form. The Brooklyn experiment established the premise that, properly counseled, selected mature adults possess needs which can be documented and programmed. Today, interestingly enough, the College Entrance Examination Board provides a testing medium of College Level Examinations which allows institutions of Higher Education to permit adults to take qualifying exams which, if passed, make possible academic placement or credit. Twenty years ago, this would have been unthinkable and suspect. Thus, we have witnessed the creation of an educational pattern; namely, adult higher education experiencing acceptance.

With this educational pattern has come the recognition of a professional area related to adult counseling. Today, this is the "sine qua non" for a sound based and timely higher education program for mature men and women. Surely the points which the authors make in this text establish a foundation as to the role and need of adult counseling. Their contributions provide a direct examination of current practices and trends.

The future of college and university adult higher education must be concerned with providing counseling services --educational, professional, and social--which recognize what adults experiences are, understand adult needs in a complex society, and relate counseling to the needs of modern society. The adult who comes to a program in higher adult education is a more capable individual than his predecessor a decade ago, granted a similar social structure and a similar motivation. In many respects, however, they are the victims of pressures and confusions which characterize a complex society. Currently we offer poor counseling services for this adult. There must be a greater awareness among the movers of higher education of the need for adequate counseling services in order that adult programs be effective instrumentalities. We need to employ all the resources available so that the adult student, man or woman, secures the best quality education and the one suited to his needs. We must assist in creating the enlightened adult: an educated person prepared for the times and the world in which he lives.

It is a truism that the future belongs to those who prepare for it. This volume, as I see it, is a conscious effort to provide information and understanding for those involved in higher education for adults, i. e., a resource instrument long overdue. Thomas Carlyle, in one of his essays, observing that conviction was an essential in life, pointed out that "Conviction without conduct is absolutely worthless." To those who read this volume and find in it a response to their convictions, it can be observed that the time and effort expended by the authors have been worthwhile. If as educators men and women related to this area will give validity to their convictions by conducting themselves in accordance, then great will be the rewards to all.

This book is a needed and valuable contribution toward translating the knowledge and skills reflected in human behavioral change that is made possible by dedicated men and women who see in adult higher education a significant area that commands attention and in a deeper sense contributes much to the well-being of our society.

Gurth I. Abercrombie

Pratt Institute
Brooklyn, New York
December, 1970

Authors in Brief

Dr. Clarence H. Thompson, Dean and Professor of Education, University College, Center for Continuing Education, Drake University; President of the Coalition of Adult Education Organizations; past President of the Association of University Evening Colleges and second Chairman of Commission XIII, American College Personnel Association.

Dr. Martha L. Farmer, Professor, Coordinator of Evening Student Personnel Services, The City College, CUNY; past Chairman of the Board of Trustees, United States Association of Evening Students and of the Adult Student Personnel Association.

Dr. Thomas O. Brown, Director of Testing and Counseling Bureau and Assistant Professor of Education, University of Akron.

Dr. Goldie Ruth Kaback, Professor of Education and Coordinator of Guidance and Counseling Program, The City College, CUNY.

Dr. Reuben R. McDaniel Jr., formerly Director of the Division of Educational Services, Baldwin-Wallace College; former member of Commission XIII and presently serving on Commission IV, American College Personnel Association and former President and Trustee of the United States Association of Evening Students.

Dr. Kenneth H. Sproull. Associate Professor of Education, Western Illinois University, Macomb, Illinois, and formerly Dean of Student Personnel Services, Lansing Community College, Lansing, Michigan.

Dr. Jean A. Rockwell, Assistant Professor, Hunter College, CUNY; former President of the Adult Student

Personnel Association and Chairman of the Board of Trustees of the United States Association of Evening Students.

Professor Jerrold I. Hirsch, Assistant Professor and Counselor of Evening Student Activities, Department of Student Personnel, Staten Island Community College, CUNY; Chairman of Commission XIII, American College Personnel Association and Trustee and past President of the Adult Student Personnel Association.

Dr. Eleanor Young Alsbrook, daughter of Dr. Whitney Young, Sr., Assistant Dean, University College, University of Louisville; formerly member of the Student Personnel Committee of the Association of University Evening Colleges and member of the American College Personnel Association.

Mrs. Beryl Warner Williams, Director of Evening and Summer Sessions and Extension Program of Morgan State College, Baltimore, Maryland; President of Maryland Association for Adult Education; Trustee, United States Association of Evening Students, and Regional Officer of the National Association of Summer Session.

Professor Hilda A. Hidalgo, Assistant Professor of Urban Studies and Social Work, Livingston College, Rutgers, the State University of New Jersey; Doctoral candidate 1971, Union Graduate School, and leader in Puerto Rican community affairs on a local, state and national level.

Dr. Mary Tatum Howard, Director of Counseling Center, Federal City College; formerly Director of Psychological Services, Kenny Rehabilitation Institute, and Assistant Professor, Augsburg College; Member-at-large of the Executive Council, American College Personnel Association, Division of the American Personnel and Guidance Association, 1971-1974 and Member of the Editorial Board of Personnel and Guidance Journal.

Chapter I

THE NATURE OF ADULT STUDENTS AND
THE SCOPE OF COUNSELING SERVICES

by Clarence H. Thompson

Introduction

In an undertaking such as the writing of a book or
even a chapter, the author makes certain assumptions about
the individuals whom he expects will read the published material. He analyzes his consumer market. He may decide
to "lecture" to them and give them the information about the
topic under consideration in a planned and organized sequence.
He may even intersperse some related personal experiences
in the hope that the presentation will be more palatable. Or
perhaps he will believe, as I do, in the concept that the
most effective learning takes place in an atmosphere of
mutual inquiry and shared interaction.

But, you might ask, how do I, the reader, dialogue
with the author after the book is in print? This technique is
one I learned from my mentor, Malcolm Knowles, of Boston
University. The reader makes a choice when picking up a
book whether he will be a passive reader or an active participant in a learning experience. The passive reader, as is
true in the case of the student who only listens to the words
of a lecturer, reads the author's presentation in the book for
information to discover his point of view.

The active learner, on the other hand, takes a ques-
tioning approach. He is somewhat skeptical of what is written and tests the author's statements and experiences against
his own understandings and experiences, accepting some,
modifying others and rejecting completely those that do not
stand up in light of this scrutiny.

A desired result of this approach is the internalizing
of the new learnings which become a part of the learner.
The principle is similar to the intake of food which is con-

sumed by the body.   Through the digestive chemical processes the food becomes energy or fat or it may be discarded as waste.   But the portion that is assimilated is no longer the same shape and size as it was when taken into the
system.   It has been modified and added to already existing
parts or systems of the body.   Likewise, the new knowledge
ingested as a result of the process of active participation in
a learning situation becomes a part of the body of knowledge
retained by the learner.   It has been subjected to a mental
processing which adds to, modifies, or replaces some of
the previously held information, concepts or understandings.

Assumptions

This chapter is not a summary of the points of view
expounded by the authors of the following chapters.   Neither
is it an attempt to catalogue the full spectrum of counseling
services available to the adult in higher education.   Rather,
I intend to deal with the unique nature of the adult who approaches institutions of higher education in an effort to
further extend his learning experiences in a direction or for
purposes of his choosing.   Additionally, I will discuss counseling services for adults on the basis of my own varied
background and experience.

Finally, I propose to explore the relationship between
counseling adults and continuing education from the points of
view of the adult counselee and the counselor.

In dealing with the topics assigned me in this chapter,
I have made certain assumptions which you, the reader, must
understand if you are to be a participant in this hopefully
learning experience.   Considering the nature of this book,
its title, the topics for the several chapters and the past
experiences resulting from an earlier related publication also edited by Martha Farmer[4], my first assumption is that
you are an adult.   Using essentially the same criteria as I
did in arriving at my first assumption, my second is not so
specific, nor so easy to state or define and in fact includes
several possible categories.   Stated briefly, my second assumption is that you are either 1) a graduate student interested in counseling or personnel work, 2) a professional in
student personnel work or counseling, or 3) an individual
adult searching for solutions to problems for which, to date,
you have been unable to locate an acceptable solution.   In
other words, you have some knowledge, understanding, experience or interest in the field of counseling.   These

assumptions in no way are intended to restrict the readers of the publication. In fact, the book should serve widely as a reference for any of the specific categories dealt with in subsequent chapters.

Nature of the Adult Student

Earlier I suggested a dialogue between us. This seems an appropriate place to begin. My first assumption is that you are an adult person. If you are reading this chapter as a part of a group, a class, several colleagues working together, or the like, let me suggest an experiment. Before you go on with your reading, get your group together and discuss the "Nature of the Adult Student" among yourselves. What is an adult? What makes him unique? Is it someone who has reached a certain age, say 18, 21 or 25 years? Or is one an adult because he has a job? Because he is the head of a household? A wife or husband? A parent? Or is it because he has left the abode of his parents? Is it because he is no longer required to attend school? Or because he can do rather as he pleases? How is he different from his counterpart, the youthful full time student? How do these differences affect his role as a student in higher education? Are these differences significant insofar as counseling is concerned? Note: If you have no group with whom to discuss these concernes, then put aside the book and make notes of your own responses before going on. Jane Zahn writes:

> Adults are not merely tall children. They differ
> from the young in many ways that influence their
> learning. They have different body characteristics,
> different learning histories, different reaction
> speed, different attitudes, values, interests, moti-
> vations, and personality. Therefore, those who
> are trying to help adults learn must be aware of
> these differences and adjust teaching and the learn-
> ing environment accordingly.[11]

In the concept of Malcolm Knowles, the difference between an adult and a youth is in this role, ranging from dependency on the one extreme to independence on the other. The more he has established his independent behavior and is able to function effectively in this role, the more adult he is considered to be.

Five differences between the adult and youth which

have important implications for higher adult education and
for college personnel services for adults, including counseling, are:

     1.   When he comes into a learning situation, the adult
has a different self-concept from the youth. The youth enters into education as a full-time vocation. It is his full-
time job. Also he has come to expect that decisions will be
made for him, that he will be told what to do, that answers
will be given to him. The adult, however, because of his
exercise of independence in other areas of his day-to-day
existence, comes to school as a means to an end. Education
is a secondary consideration and, therefore, the adult's expectations are different. Also the adult wants to be treated
as an adult and to make his own decisions. He doesn't want
to be talked down to and have everything decided for him.
He expects to take some responsibility and to have the opportunity to participate. In view of his experiences with
education as a youth, though, he develops an ambivalence
since he expects that decisions will be made for him, that
he will be talked down to and that the teachers will tell him
what he ought to do. One of the important tasks for counselors of adults becomes helping the classroom teachers and
the adult students to understand these differences.

     2.   Since an adult has lived longer than a youth, the
adult has had more experience. This is important to recognize in a learning situation. Since the adult has more experience than the youth, he has more to contribute to certain
learning situations. The instruction should be more experi-
entially oriented and take advantage of the many involvement
techniques available.

     3.   An adult differs from youth in that an adult enters
into a learning environment to attain the immediate use of
what he learns; to help in the solution of immediate life
problems. Youth enters with the idea of postponed use of
learnings. He is storing up knowledge for the time when he
becomes an adult and becomes a full-time wage earner. Consequently, he is oriented to subject matter. The adult enters
the educational environment looking for solutions to his day-
to-day problems and becomes oriented to problem-centered or
problem-solving objectives.

     4.   Somewhat related to the previous difference for
the adult is the effect that certain stages of his development
have upon his educational desires. His reasons for turning

to education usually relate to the nature of the problems con-
fronting him. These habitually conform to the three major
periods of development of his adult years, early, middle and
later maturity. In his early adulthood, he is more likely to
be concerned with courses dealing with how to get a job and
to do it better; how to deal with problems in family living;
marriage; child rearing; money management; how to communicate, relate and socialize with new groupings of friends,
neighbors, and co-workers, and how to be an effective and
responsible mature citizen. In his middle years, he will
primarily be concerned with his professional or vocational
success; of getting ahead. He may develop additional cultural tastes, become interested in the later stages of child
development and/or update some of his earlier skills or
understandings. During the later years, he is more likely
to desire sessions that will contribute to the use of leisure
time; preparation for or living in retirement and some way
of remaining useful after 65 with areas of broadened interests.

    5. A fifth difference is in the category of motivation;
i. e. , reasons for going to school. Youth is required to attend school by law and, also, by pressures from parents,
friends and peers. Usually it is the "in" thing to do. Adults
go because they want to; because they feel some sense of
inadequacy; because of new employment or promotion possibilities or to learn about some new skill, language, or interest. Since usually they are motivated to achieve, they
tend to withdraw from and to resent poor teaching and faculty who repeat their 50-minute sessions from day classes. [9]

    With an understanding of the nature of the adult stu-
dent and his differences from the youthful student, it is
then a series of small steps for student personnel workers
and administrators to utilize this knowledge in assisting
adults to overcome frustrations and to get maximum results
from educational experiences.

Scope of Counseling Services

    Colleges and universities have increasingly given at-
tention to the needs and interests of the full-time youthful
student and his problems. Professional groups of personnel
workers have advocated increased facilities and services for
students for several years. Yet on most campuses today
there are still inadequate facilities and too few trained, professional, student personnel staff to meet the needs of the

increasing numbers of youthful full-time students. Promotional materials and catalogues indicate services that sound elaborate and complete. Yet look at the attrition--the dropouts, the failures, the misfits; look at the academic and emotional problems which arise, and the numbers of students who never make proper adjustments. These are but some evidences of the fact that even for the youthful student, personnel services, including counseling, are far from Utopian.

In those publications describing adult programs, such as evening college catalogues, reference is usually made to the availability of advising or counseling. Unfortunately, the service is frequently exaggerated. For example, in one evening college catalogue which I had occasion to look at recently, the statement was made that "counseling is available evenings by appointment. " Also it went on to state that nonmatriculated students without an assigned advisor were encouraged to seek counseling. Sounds great! Also it was technically true. One counselor was available by appointment two nights per week from 6 to 8:30 p. m. Figuring half an hour per client this amounts to a maximum of ten students per week who can be accommodated. Considering only the nonmatriculated students, it would take perfect scheduling for two years, 50 weeks per year, for each student to have one 30-minute period of counseling.

Some institutions have only daytime hours available for appointments and the counseling staff considers it an imposition to spend time with a night adult student. Of course, these are extreme cases but they are real. Although there are a number of institutions that do as much, or more, for the adult as they do for the full-time youth, in many institutions it is counseling for adults that leaves much room for improvement.

It is again time for dialogue. But first one additional bit of input seems appropriate before you begin your deliberations. With the adult in mind, a working definition of "counseling" was developed by a participant group at a conference on "The Training of Counselors of Adults" held at Chatham, Massachusetts, in May 1965. As given to me by a participant, it states

> Counseling is a systematic exploration of self and/ or environment by a client with the aid of a counselor to clarify self-understandings and/or environmental alternatives so that behavior modifications

or decisions are made on the basis of greater cognitive and affective understandings.

In commenting upon this definition, Goldie Kaback states

> This definition assumes that the adult is sufficiently
> independent and responsible for himself and perhaps
> for others, to be able to develop a plan of action
> during the counseling process that can be actualized
> without the mitigating influences of those who feel
> themselves responsible for his welfare and adjust-
> ment. [5]

Now, is your group available? In looking at the scope
of counseling services for adults in higher education, how
should they be classified or categorized? Should we think
of the spectrum of services that are available in those institutions which are doing the most for their adult students?
Should we attempt to design a model of services for most
universities to strive to develop? If so, what should be considered essential services, desirable services, and ideal
services? If not, then how best to consider this section of
the assignment?

Having developed your criteria and approach, let us
now compare notes. My considerations led me to decide
upon two separate listings. The first, I would refer to as
functional categories. In this way, we will consider the
function to be served by the counseling and arbitrarily de-
lineate segments with names. Let me illustrate my categories of educational, professional or vocational, and personal counseling (including referral):

One function in the setting we are considering, counseling services for adults in higher education, and perhaps
the one most widespread in use and availability, is educational counseling. Broadly viewed, this function might include program and course advising, group guidance and
orientation, aids in overcoming learning difficulties such as
programmed learning materials, remedial courses, or reading and study skills. It also may include testing of aptitudes, interests, abilities, achievement, or social and emotional attitudes. The student may be referred to the counsel-
or by a faculty member or an administrator. The student
also should be counseled promptly when he comes of his own
volition. Educational counseling is the functional area in
which many counselors of adults have the most knowledge
and understanding.

A second function is <u>professional</u> or vocational counseling. This is the bridge <u>connecting educational counseling</u>
on the one bank with personal counseling on the other. It
serves as a link which unites them into a single working
whole. As is true of most bridges, the approaches are
long and extend partly over the land on each end. Just as
on a bridge it is difficult to determine where the land ends
and the water begins, so it is difficult to distinguish specifically the beginning and ending of the overlapping areas between educational, personal and professional counseling. The
materials from which this bridge of professional counseling
has been constructed include: vocational counseling, career
information, placement, occupational information, testing for
vocational purposes, periodic growth assessment, and long-
range counseling aimed at the attainment of maximum self-
fulfillment for the individual.

The third function of <u>personal</u> counseling is not as
easily discernible as the <u>previous two</u>. An expressed educational concern or the seeking of assistance in selecting a
career might easily be only the symptom of the adult's problem. He might have a personal problem that he hasn't
recognized or refuses to admit. Much of the time the client
will express an educational or professional problem to the
counselor. It is only later in the session that an empathetic
counselor may discover that the basis for seeking help is
really in the category of personal problems.

It is essential that the counselor know his capabilities
and his limitations. Some problems may be so deep-rooted
as to require psychiatric help over a period of time. The
counselor needs to be sufficiently skilled to recognize these
situations where referral is indicated. Obviously, he needs
to know what resources are available to him for this purpose.
No professional counselor will risk the well-being and mental
health of his client. He will make a referral if the situation
appears to be beyond the limits of his background and training.

These divisions are arbitrary and in actual practice
do not exist as a neat package. An educational problem may
have vocational aspects and also personal implications. For
example, a student may want to take a course in personnel
work because his boss suggested it and because he has been
moved into a new position. His family may resent the additional nights away from home life and the use of scarce financial resources to pay for tuition and books. Essentially
an educational problem, there are elements of the other segments, too.

For the second listing of categories I have selected
four client groups. These are not intended to be inclusive.
Several of those that are the subject of separate chapters,
I have omitted.

The first of these client categories I refer to as
part-time credit-oriented adults. This group perhaps represents the largest number of adult students who regularly
use the counseling services of the institutions of higher
learning. They might be called the evening college students
or degree-seeking or matriculated students but each of these
latter terms is too restrictive. The part-time credit-oriented adult includes all of these and more. As the terminolo-
gy implies, a goal orientation of these adults is academic
credit. They may be in search of a degree; a certificate;
a credit course for possible future use or for transfer to
another institution; updating knowledge; or a skill; or perhaps just to meet the reimbursement requirements of an employer who encouraged a particular learning activity.

Counseling services for these adults may include advising, program-planning, registration assistance, testing
for admissions, placement or achievement, financial and
scholarship assistance; or, remedial help such as reading
and study skills, preparatory English, or mathematics; or,
professional or vocational information and selection, job
interviewing, résumé preparation; or just academic difficulties and probation or personal problems. The problems of
health, alcoholism, drug use and abuse, rehabilitation, psychiatric counseling, legal counsel, religion, pre-marital,
marriage and family counseling and other similar areas of
concern will usually be referred for specialized professional
assistance.

A second client category I refer to as the pre-retirement and retirement group. These persons, faced with the
advent of more leisure time at their disposal, either now or
in the forseeable future, are likely to turn to education primarily for one of two reasons. First, they want to know
about those things in life which retirement will cause to be
different. Among this segment of their interests are included a desire for information regarding social security
benefits, medicaid and medicare, wills, legal and financial
information, continuing education and the identification of
elements of fulfillment during post-retirement years such
as vocational, avocational, seasonal or other uses of leisure
time. Second, the retired adult may turn to education for

the pleasure of learning, to keep his mental processes alert, to broaden his knowledge about a specific subject, or to create vicarious experiences.

A retirement revolution currently is causing significant changes in both the dimensions and the nature of retirement. The number of older adults who are retiring and living for 20 to 30 years in retirement is increasing dramatically. Note, for example, that earlier retirement is becoming a reality for many. The impact that medical science has had on increasing the life span is evident when one thinks about progress in controlling and curing major diseases. The increasing availability of organ transplants and miracle drugs, together with medicare for most retirees, will increase the healthful years further.

In Washington, D. C. during public hearings before the Subcommittee on Retirement and the Individual of the Senate Special Committee on Aging, Senator Walter F. Mondale, the chairman, in his opening statement on June 7, 1967, indicated that his committee is studying "the institution of retirement itself and of its impact on the individual, especially as regards the problems of adjusting to a new role in life and the need for meaning and fulfillment in the retirement years."[8] In testifying before this same committee, John Gardner, then Secretary of Health, Education, and Welfare, said

> ... despite a good deal of progress in recent years, one of the most serious defects in our present arrangement for older people is the absence of relevant and useful things for them to do, whether this be paid work or a personal activity. Like everyone else, older people need to be needed. They need to have something to occupy their hands and minds and hearts. [8]

Drake University with the aid of a three-year government grant, conducted a demonstration project called the Retirement Opportunity Planning Center (also referred to as the Retirement Center and the Pre-Retirement Center). This Retirement Center tested various approaches to recruitment, counseling, and active involvement in broad areas of concern for pre-retirees: 1) legal and financial, 2) health and welfare, 3) continuing education, and 4) identification of appropriate roles for post-retirement years.

More than a thousand individuals attended programs aimed at better equipping them to make intelligent, informed decisions about retirement and suggesting roles and activities leading to a satisfying and creative retirement. Intended to include participants ranging in age from 50 to 65, recruiting developed primarily in two directions. Four target groups included industrial workers, white collar employees of large agencies, government employees, and professionals. These groups were generally served at the place of employment on a time sharing basis, i.e., an hour of company time and an hour of the employee's time for each of the seven sessions. The second direction of service was for individuals from the community at large. They were recruited by newspaper advertisement and usually met at the Center at night. Spouses were encouraged to attend the activities and counseling sessions also.

In commenting on the program in Active Times the director stated

> Participants look with increased interest at recreational opportunities and continued education. Even before their retirement, they consult lawyers about their wills, financial advisors about their money, doctors about their health. They learn more about retirement housing and part-time work possibilities and reassess their plans accordingly. By the attendance of husband and wife fears and problems which may have been privately nourished are brought to light and reduced through sharing. [1]

Some institutions offer reduced or free tuition to retirees, making it possible for many to continue their educational interests. Although many of the activities and problems of major concern to retirees are not usually a part of the programs of institutions of higher learning, counselors should be cognizant of the resources available for proper referral.

A third client category that needs some special comment I have termed "adult women." It is true that in each of the previous categories, a large number of the clients are women. This category considers those problems which relate to the housewife-mother who has lived a discontinuous life. She is likely to approach the institution or counselor in search of reassurance, advice or information as to what her alternatives are in the world outside the home.

She probably has finished high school, has had some college several years ago or, in increasing number, she may be a college graduate.

Her first concern is likely to be whether or not she can compete favorably with the younger students. This comes out in many ways. "I've been out of school 15 years. Do you think I'm too old to learn?" "After years of talking to a preschooler, I don't know if I can carry on an adult conversation anymore." "I had two years of college 20 years ago but my grades were only fair. Do you think I'm foolish to try again?" "I wasn't very good in math or science so don't you think I ought to start with those?" "My family are all leaving me behind. I want to find out if I'm as stupid as they think I am." These and other deep concerns about her abilities have been expressed by hundreds of women in my experience as an adult counselor and administrator. The first hurdle seems to be one of lack of confidence.

Another difficulty for many of this group, which is perhaps related, is that she does not get feedback in her home and family environment regarding her intellectual abilities. She hasn't anything against which to compare them. An educational experience can help her evaluate her abilities as well as determine her goals and objectives and get her started toward their attainment.

Many universities and colleges have developed programs of continuing education for women--in excess of two hundred at last count. Guidance and counseling plays a significant role in nearly all of them. For instance, at a conference on women called by the governor of New York on May 26 and 27, 1966, Dr. Esther Westervelt proposed the following services be included in the first of a series of Guidance Centers for Women:

> Individual professional counseling on education, jobs, and goals; testing of interests, aptitudes, and personal needs; group counseling to explore personal goals; periodic group guidance courses on paid and unpaid job opportunities, home management, consumer education, organization and community leadership; and publications and continuing public information on new educational and occupational opportunities and the services available at the center. [3]

There has been "an appraisal of the New York State Guidance
Center for Women" published in 1970. [2]

The fourth client category, I have designated as "career development adults. " Some of these may well be included in subsequent chapters but not as a total group. My
use of "career development adults" refers to those individuals
who are participants in specific government supported programs conducted by institutions under contract. These include New Careers, Occupational Upgrading Programs, Public Service Careers, many Model Cities programs, and some
Employment Security training programs.

They have in common a form of assessment of the
participants before enrollment, small classes, tutorial assistance, courses in generic issues of human services and
deferred college credit. The participants usually will not,
at the beginning, meet the normal admission standards of
the institution. Experience, however, as a result of the
sheltered courses, indicates that of those enrolled, about
80 per cent succeed insofar as job satisfactions are concerned and better than 50 per cent succeed academically.

In addition to the similarities listed above, the regis-
trants in these programs have regularly scheduled sessions
with qualified counselors who work only with these individuals.
Input from employers of the attendees is provided through
the training coordinators who serve as an active liaison between the university, the contractors, the employer and the
participant.

New Career-ists come from poverty-level unemployed
persons. Occupational Upgrading is restricted to heads of
households in the model cities area but is not confined to
the poverty income level. Other contracts specify the guidelines for participation but generally are aimed at improving
the employability of those who successfully complete the
program.

One rather unique exception is the contract program
which Drake University is conducting in conjunction with the
Iowa Employment Security Commission. The participants
in this program were selected from the employees of Employment Security. In general, they were para-professionals
who had been hired by offices throughout the state to work
with the hard-core unemployed, the handicapped, the alco-
holic, the incarcerated, and the economically and culturally

deprived. The program, through a series of four two-week institutes, is to help find solutions for dealing with these difficult-to-place clients. One of the key segments of the program includes group guidance and counseling techniques.

From a counseling service point of view, this client category presents a different spectrum of problems from the others. Many socially disadvantaged people are accepting the importance of education for job and economic successes. Their past experience has been frustration, failure and poverty of mind and environment. A concept different from the traditional methods of counseling, teaching and job developing is needed. The program emphasized change of attitudes, self-concepts, human behavior and the development of communications skills.

But central to any program for this type of adult student is the continual availability of appropriate, professionally trained counselors.

Continuing Education and Counseling Services

Do you have your group? What does continuing education have to do with counseling services? What is meant by continuing education? Assuming that there is some reason for this section, how would you treat this topic?

I spent some time deciding upon an approach, just as you did in miniature. I tested different ideas and discarded some, just as you no doubt did. You could say that "counseling services" for the adult should enhance his efforts in continuing his education--and you would be right. You could suggest that the development of counselors through continuing education would contribute to better counseling for the adult-- and you would also be right. You might consider the role of continuing education in the development of the student or you could look at the student's development, up or down, by using or avoiding continuing education. Or you might consider the adult's success or lack thereof in his continuing education endeavors, with or without counseling. I suspect that nearly anything you thought of by using the terms in concert has contributed to your own learning experience.

It is a well-worn cliché that in today's complex and technologically-oriented society, a person can no longer be educated for life but must continue his education throughout life--hence the expression "lifelong learning." If we look at

continuing education as lifelong learning, then it becomes evident that learning is a social process that involves the total
personality of the learner.   Malcolm Knowles, in a faculty
development meeting at Drake University stated, "the time
span of cultural revolution is now less than the lifetime of
a human being.   We are now living in a time where the
present adult generation is faced with managing a culture
different in kind from the one originally transmitted to
them. "[7]

It is obvious that adults attending institutions of higher
learning are continuing their education.   However, all continuing education is not necessarily conducted on campuses.
Perhaps not quite so obvious is the necessity for counselors
to be aware of the resources available to adults who desire
to continue their education.   Just as expectations from the
learning situation are different because of his different concept of his role, so are the needs, problems and concerns
different for which he will seek a counselor.

In looking at the relationship of counseling services
to continuing education, let me suggest that continuing education is really the unifying theme, the basic fabric, upon
which college personnel services, including counseling, can
and should become effective for the adult.   For the personnel worker or counselor, participation in a meaningful plan
of continuing his own education is essential.

> Nothing becomes old so quickly as the skin of a
> dead sheep, yet there are those graduates who
> expect their diploma to keep their minds alive
> forever.   The challenge of change, the enthusiasm
> of seeking satisfactory solutions to life's problems,
> the spirit of helpful service may well be good moti-
> vators, but only through continuing one's education
> can he become really effective. [10]

Although the following chapters have not been written
with the idea of dialoging with you, the reader, may I suggest that you continue this learning experience by developing
your own questions as you progress through the book.   Now
in closing this chapter let me ask you one final question.
Did you learn from this experience?

References

1. Active Times, Des Moines, Iowa: Drake University
   Pre-Retirement Planning Center, September 1969.

2. An Appraisal of the New York State Guidance Center
   for Women, State University of New York, 1970,
   155 pp & xv.

3. Conference on Women: Proceedings of Governor Rocke-
   feller's Conference on Women, Albany, N. Y., 1966,
   pp 6-7.

4. Farmer, Martha L., ed., Student Personnel Services
   for Adults in Higher Education, Metuchen, N. J. :
   Scarecrow Press, 1967.

5. Kaback, Goldie R., "Implications for Counseling the
   Adult," in Clarence H. Thompson, ed., Counseling
   the Adult Student, Des Moines, Iowa: Drake University, 1967, p. 13.

6. Knowles, Malcolm S., The Modern Practice of Adult
   Education: Andragogy Versus Pedagogy, New York:
   Association Press, 1970.

7. Knowles, Malcolm S., The Adult Education Movement
   in the United States, New York: Holt, Rinehart and
   Winston, 1962.

8. Retirement and the Individual. Hearings before the Sub-
   committee on Retirement and the Individual of the
   Special Committee on Aging, United States Senate,
   Ninetieth Congress, Part I, Survey Hearing, Wash-
   ington, D. C., June 7 and 8, 1967. Washington:
   U. S. Government Printing Office, 1967.

9. Thompson, Clarence H., "Admission and Counseling of
   Adult Students" in Asa S. Knowles, ed., Handbook
   of College and University Administration, New York:
   McGraw-Hill, 1970, 2 vols, pp. 5-19-34.

10. Thompson, Clarence H., ed., College Personnel Serv-
    ices for the Adult, Des Moines, Iowa: Drake Univer-
    sity, 1968, p. 22.

11. Zahn, Jane C., "Differences Between Adults and Youth
    Affecting Learning" in Adult Edication, Volume XVII
    No. 2, Winter 1967, p. 67.

Chapter II

COUNSELING ADULTS IS DIFFERENT

by Martha L. Farmer

The current recommendations for re-structuring higher education to include the adults whom the system had virtually excluded, are particularly relevant to psychological counseling. There is a plethora of books, studies and research dealing with the psychological counseling of the usual undergraduate student. Little has been written or researched in this area as it applies to the adult in higher education.

One of the most frequently asked questions concerning adult counseling is the manner in which it differs from counseling adolescent college students. There are undoubtedly continuities between the two. However, there are many differences. It is the purpose of this chapter to attempt to clarify some of these dissimilarities. A major difficulty has been in arriving at a workable definition of an adult. The following definition will be used throughout this chapter.

> An adult is an essentially self-sustaining and/or socially independent person, regardless of chronological age, as he is regarded by society and self as fulfilling an adult role. [10]

There are three basic areas which should be considered as they relate to the adult: age, psychological maturity, and social role.

Age

Many aspects of age have come to be almost meaningless due to the variety of legal definitions used by local, state and federal governments. A longitudinal approach which considers the adult's abilities changing with age, as demonstrated by a series of studies of adult learning, can best serve our purpose.

The early studies, World War I's Army Alpha Test for example, and those subsequently conducted in 1928 by Thorndike and his associates, set the peak adult learning years as 21 to 22. Thereafter his potentiality declined at a steady rate until the age of approximately 42 to 60. The early standardization of the Wechsler-Bellevue which used a cross-sectional test design supported these findings. The 1955 standardization of this test moved the peak performance years to 25 to 29. The adult's ability declined thereafter at a steady rate. [3]

These research results have been challenged by Lorge and others. They found that standardized tests are not a true measure of adult learning ability. Physiologically, his reaction time may become slower with age, but this does not mean that he is unable to learn. Pressey found that the cultural bias of tests favored the in-school youth and ignored the motivations and problems of adult learning. [4]

The adult has multi-dimensional abilities which do not appear when tested on a single measurement. The adult's test-profiles show variables due to his uneven scores on sub-tests. It has become evident that the adult possesses many skills not yet quantified. The latest research work in this area, being conducted by Kingsley Wientge of the University of Missouri at St. Louis, demonstrates that new measures must be devised and standardized for adults to measure their academic ability. Several recent recommendations by task forces and commissions suggest that life experience be evaluated in terms of academic credit. This type of evaluation would be particularly appropriate for adults entering and/or returning to higher education.

Psychological Maturity

Psychological maturity is difficult to gauge, as a person may be psychologically mature at 18 and immature at 60. Perhaps by considering the concept of differentiation, we may find some clues. "As a person moves through the adult years, there is a diversification of abilities, skills, attitudes, interests, etc. , within the individual, and in the course of social interaction, a similar diversification in relation to other persons. "[5] The adult's potential can be realized through clarifying and defining preferences which have grown out of practice and experience.

Howard McClusky says, "Disposition, stance, set or

whatever term one prefers, denotes characteristics especially relevant for understanding the psychology of adult behavior. "[8]

The adult's set "is a function of habit and the Law of Least Effort. " He tends to repeat behavioral patterns even though they may be less effective than other ways of responding. His particular set is influenced by his preoccupation with what he has known and his feelings about his ways of reacting. As he becomes progressively older physiologically, there is a slowing down of his reaction time to new stimuli. The adult is selective in responding to experiences which he wishes to organize and retain. A disadvantage may be the tendency to use what is known, rather than to react to new possibilities for action. It may also limit his ability to perceive effective alternatives. [9]

An adult characteristic is his integrative response to the continuous experience he accumulates with age. In our present day culture, with its many demands, these stimuli may be overwhelming to the adult if he does not react in a discriminating manner. He must reduce these demands to manageable terms if he is to maintain his autonomy and protect his ego. "The use of the word integrative stresses the point that the process of selective incorporation is never complete, but like breathing, is in constant operation as a condition for maintenance of autonomy. "[6]

Social Role

The adult's social roles increase along an age-time continuum. Cultural expectations set certain roles which the adult must assume as he moves through the age-time zone. The psychological time-future is tenuous to a child, vague but unlimited to an adolescent and realistic to the adult. In the middle years, at 40 one year would represent one-fortieth of the time the adult has known. His time continuum goes, not only back to the experiences he has had, but also stretches into the unknown future. The rationalizations of these time factors may be a traumatic experience to some adults. Many times they do not know how to cope with the slowing down of physiological functions, planning for retirement and change of role in the family constellation. This is one period during which the adult may seek psychological counseling. It is, therefore, apparent that sensitivity to the age-time factor and reaction to its variables is an important feature of adult psychology.

Another aspect of time is related to the "career-sequence perceived by persons at various positions in the occupational hierarchy. "[7]   The mobility of our present day society has made former career sub-limits less predictable than they were 50 years ago.   Today, the farmer's son may have greater career aspirations than following in his father's footsteps.   The children of the blue-collar workers may, through education, move into the white-collar or professional ranks.   The children of the white-collar or professional workers may even opt out of established society and join one of the common cults or movements.

The mobility of the general population into different geographical locales of employment and re-employment may have a marked effect on the adult as he progresses through his role-time continuum.   These moves may pose a greater threat to the adult's autonomy at some ages than at others. The lack of this mobility due to culturally imposed restrictions could well become a source of increasing alienation and frustration to minority groups.   All of these societal thrusts point out the need of a broad psycho-social basis for adult counseling.

Adult Counseling

The forms adult counseling may take vary "from information-giving to deeper psychological and personal re-orientations. "[11]   The stresses of today's society have created a need on the part of many adults to seek counseling.   This need will increase as our society becomes more complex.

In counseling, an adult must come to grips with his self-concept, abilities, potentialities, roles he must play and defenses he requires to protect his autonomy.   Important aspects of his adjustment to society are the environment within which he operates: its opportunities, restrictions, and possible change of restrictions.   The adult has a greater independence, sense of responsibility and a longer life-history than does the adolescent.   The adult, because he has lived longer "has more knowledge, whether accurate or not, and at least part of this knowledge is about himself and his own life history. "[13]   The adult may be aided by the counselor to use this knowledge in a new perspective.

The adult may not have the same reaction to counseling and the counselor as does the adolescent.   Because of his life history, he will respond to the situation in terms of

his own experiences.   If his responsibilities have been restrictive, he may tend to protect and defend his autonomy,
values, roles and time-prospective.   If his personal history
has a positive connotation, he may have greater potential
for action.   This may be directly related to the way in
which he solved his problems of independence and ego protection.

The adult knows more about himself and, therefore,
does not have to "learn about himself" in the same way as
does the adolescent.   He may, however, not have been able
to put the pieces together because of his inability to conceptu-
alize.   His decisions must be consistent with his commitment
pattern.   The adolescent, because of his fewer years of living, may have more choices of direction. [12] Maslow says
the counselor must help the adult toward "A more satisfying
life, in the client's own life-style by making use of existing
capacities so that he can be more fully what he is potential-
ly. "[1]

Group therapy often lends itself to assist in resolving
adult problems which do not benefit from a one-to-one relationship.   It could provide adults, who have resources within
themselves, an alternate way of dealing with their needs.
Many groups such as Alcoholics Anonymous, Weight Watchers,
Gamblers Anonymous and others have used this type of therapy to provide support and aid in the resolution of their members' problems.   It is suggested that some adults feel more
comfortable in a group situation when they realize that other
group members have similar difficulties.   The anonymity of
group membership may decrease fear of public exposure.   In
a counseling situation, it would not be inappropriate for the
psychologist to suggest this as an alternative course of action.
He could also suggest possible resource persons to meet with
the group if the need should arise. [14]

Counselors in the setting of higher education are
generally more familiar with the psychology of the adolescent
and the late adolescent than they are with that of the adult.
Many tend to base their counseling on the continuities of
problems shared by these groups rather than taking into consideration the very real differences.   Younger counselors
may be psychologically ill-equipped to deal with the variety
of adult real-life problems.   The problems the adult brings
to the college counseling office run the gamut of human difficulties.   The training and background of the psychologist
must be extensive enough to enable him to relate to the

middle-aged and older client with real empathy.   Without
this rapport, the counseling session may well become an
exercise in futility.

Much of our knowledge of adult psychology has been
derived from dealing with highly articulate clients.   There
are many areas of adult counseling about which we have little knowledge.   The response of minority group members to
the counseling process is an area which needs a great deal
of investigation and research.   The foreign-born whose life-
styles and cultural expectations are quite different from ours,
often cannot be aided by counseling because this kind of one-
to-one relationship is not found in his culture.   We need to
know more about his life pattern and his personal hierarchies.
It is hoped that with the expansion of counseling services for
adults, we will gain further knowledge in these areas.

Conclusion

The short discussion of differences between adult and
adolescent counseling psychology in this chapter is not meant
to be definitive in nature.   Its purpose is merely to discuss
briefly some of the more salient differences.   A great deal
more meaningful research must be conducted if we are to
truly serve the adult client who seeks counseling.

Maslow said:

> The far goals for adult education, and for other
> education, are to find the processes, the ways in
> which we can help people become all they are
> capable of becoming ....   To help the client
> achieve such intrinsic learning is the far goal
> of counseling. [2]

References

1.   Maslow, Abraham, The New England Board of Higher
     Education and The Center for The Study of Liberal
     Education for Adults, Proceedings of the Conference
     on the Training of Counselors of Adults, Chatham,
     Mass., May, 1965, p. 170.

2.   Ibid., p. 205.

3. McClusky, Howard Y., "The Relevance of Psychology for Adult Education," in Jensen, G., Liveright, A. A., and Hallenbeck, W., eds., Adult Education: Outlines of an Emerging Field of University Study, Adult Education Association of the U.S.A., 1964, p. 162.

4. Ibid., p. 163.

5. Ibid., p. 156.

6. Ibid., p. 159.

7. Ibid., p. 161.

8. Ibid., p. 158.

9. Ibid., p.

10. Maslow, op. cit., p. 169.

11. Ibid., p. 170.

12. Ibid., p.

13. Ibid., p.

14. Ibid., p. 195.

Chapter III

COUNSELING ADULTS WITH EDUCATIONAL PROBLEMS

by Thomas O. Brown

The first step in the discussion of counseling services for adults with educational problems is to define what is meant by "educational" problems and to illustrate the significance of this problem area in higher education.

Diagnostic classification in counseling has been treated with varying degrees of interest over the past 30 to 35 years. Early in the history of counseling, diagnosis was generally accepted as a legitimate part of the counseling process. [6, 35, 42] Then, with the emphasis on Rogerian techniques and philosophy, diagnosis faded into the background as a part of the counseling process. However, in the past several years, the role of diagnosis has become the subject of increased emphasis and investigation. Although the question of need for diagnosis has promoted energetic discussion, both pro and con, in professional literature, a number of authors have made a case for the use of diagnosis in the counseling process. [4, 5, 11, 12, 39, 41]

According to English and English, diagnosis may be defined as "any classification of an individual on the basis of observed character."[17] Williamson and Darley describe one of the earliest diagnostic classification systems using the following problem categories: vocational, educational, personal-social-emotional, financial, health and family. [42] Others have modified, refined, and built upon this early classification system in attempting to define different psychological difficulties and to establish treatment procedures for handling the problem. Most of these diagnostic classifications' systems have included the category of educational problems.

Williamson and Darley group the following signs of student maladjustment under the educational problem area:

discrepancies between achievements and abilities; discrepancies between ambitions and abilities; discrepancies between claimed and measured interest; discrepancies between measured interest and ability; poor study habits; indecision; specific deficiencies such as reading disabilities, spelling weaknesses, inadequacies in mathematics and related areas; inappropriate perspectives on education; lack of motivation; lack of skill in use of aptitudes and plans limited by educational red tape. [42]

The Missouri Diagnostic Classification Plan describes educational problems as involving "lack of effective study skills and habits, poor reading ability or lack of information about institutional policies and regulations. Primarily concerned with adjustment to current situations rather than planning for future. "[12]

Educational counseling is also outlined in some detail by Rackham in his Student Personnel Services Inventory. The purpose of the inventory is to "assist colleges and universities in evaluating their programs of student personnel services. "[36] Educational counseling is described by Rackham as a major type of student problem and includes the following general areas: accurately appraising aptitudes; discovering abilities; selecting and making progress in appropriate courses of study; conforming to academic machinery; understanding curriculum; mechanics of course requirements; contents of courses; special programs; characteristics; abilities necessary for success; faculty regulations and idiosyncrasies of departments and instructors; and so on. [36]

In one of very few discussions of educational counseling for adults, Fisher defines educational counseling as "counseling for overcoming educational handicaps. "[19] He goes on to describe educational handicaps as "training or skill deficiencies of an academic sort which make further learning in a particular area unnecessarily difficult, unlikely or even impossible.... In educational counseling the central focus is on learning difficulties centered around formal educational processes. "[19]

Because of the variety of educational problems, and the diverse background, orientation and work setting of those who provide help to adults with these problems, the approaches may also be quite different. Some of these approaches could be described as counseling, while others could more accurately be defined as advisement. Although overlapping

exists, some distinction should be made between these two
approaches. The definition of counseling as developed at
the Chatham Conference is helpful in differentiating counseling from advisement and information giving.

> Counseling is a systematic exploration of self and/
> or environment with the aid of a counselor to
> clarify self-understanding and/or environmental
> alternatives so that behavior modification or de-
> cisions are made on the basis of greater cognitive
> and affective understanding. [31]

Although the educational counseling process may involve advisement or information-giving "... the work counselor is preferably restricted to professionally trained persons. ... Unfortunately both noun and verb, counsel, retain
an old meaning of advice-giving which is now conceived as
only part of the counseling process. "[15]

In a pioneer publication on student personnel services
for adults in higher education, Palais provides the following
observation. "A distinction should be made between advisement and counseling.... Advisement is what the term implies, i. e. , the giving of information or advice in any area
and on any subject. "[34]

He goes on to explain that advising includes curriculum and course selection, substitution, evaluation and transfer of credits and other topics dealing with one's courses of
study. However, topics relating to academic performance,
especially if probation or dismissal may be involved, should
be handled by a professional counselor because of the relationship between poor academic performance and other problems.

In the same publication Braund also differentiates the
counseling and advising roles. He describes advising as providing suggestions, directions or information, whereas in
counseling, behavior change is achieved primarily through
insight and self-recognition. [8]

The area of educational counseling has been generally
recognized as an appropriate counseling service to be offered in the higher education setting. Oetting uses the categories of "academic counseling" and "academic services" in
reporting a study of problems and issues in the administration of college and university counseling services. [33] Nugent

and Pareis in their survey of policies and practices in college counseling centers found that 67 per cent of the centers
responding to the questionnaire indicated that help with "reading and study habits" was offered. [32]   Clark found that 85
per cent of the counseling centers in 36 major universities
offer "academic and educational counseling."[15]

The Ohio State University Counseling Center goes beyond many university counseling services in providing a
specific learning and reading skills service for clients.
This service is described on the Center intake form as including counseling for concerns such as: improving reading
and other skills, difficulty in understanding textbooks, lectures, instructors, improving ability to concentrate on studies, improving ability to prepare for and take exams, not
enough time for study and/or recreation, taking uninterest-
ing courses, and improving organization of study and use of
time.

The University of Akron Testing and Counseling
Bureau, in an informational brochure, describes educational
counseling as including achieving a better balance between
academic life and social life, developing greater interest
and self-discipline in academic work, understanding the relationship between courses of study and personal goals and
objectives, understanding the relationship between abilities
and academic success, and understanding factors contributing to choice of a major field of study and the development
of effective study habits and skills.

Types of Educational Problems of Adults

Because the adult in the higher education setting differs in a number of ways from the student in the normal
college-age range, his educational problems also differ in
several ways from the educational-academic problems of the
younger student.   Some of the more common educational
problems of adults are described as follows:

1. Poor educational background.   Many adults have
either a weak high school-college preparatory background,
or have been out of school for so many years that whatever
academic background they did possess may be of limited
value to them in their current educational program.   A
large number of adults would have a much better chance at
success if they took the time for developmental or remedial

courses in basic skill areas such as English, Mathematics and Reading Comprehension before placing themselves in what might be a highly competitive classroom situation with younger students who have not been out of school as long and who may have a superior educational background.

2. Inadequate study skills.   Another common weakness of the adult student is the lack of effective study methods and techniques.   Even the adult who may have done well in high school or his first year or so of college but who may have been out of school for a number of years may well require a review of basic considerations in efficient and effective study habits such as organizing and planning for study, improving reading ability and techniques for studying textbook assignment, improving ability to concentrate and memorize, and taking notes and preparing for and taking examinations.

3. Lack of confidence.   The first two problem areas mentioned, poor educational background and ineffective study skills, whether real or imaginary, contribute to a general feeling of anxiety and fear of failure in the academic setting. Many younger students, just entering college, are fearful, frustrated, and often discouraged at being constantly reminded of the so-called "knowledge explosion" that has become a favorite topic of individuals prominent in government, business and industry, and education.   With the "new math, " "new chemistry, " "new social studies, " and "new" almost everything else, it is not surprising that the adult who has been out of school for a number of years and who may look back on a rather basic educational background, feels a great deal of anxiety and fear at the enormous task facing him. If he is not careful, the adult may find himself defeated before he really begins, if he is not given accurate information about the requirements of his educational program and his ability to satisfactorily meet these requirements.   The counselor may have to provide a good bit of support until the individual has had an opportunity to prove to himself that he can succeed in this new and challenging situation.

4. Unrealistic expectations.   One aspect of this problem is related very closely to lack of confidence.   The individual who lacks confidence has a tendency to have an unrealistically low aspiration level and to establish objectives or goals which are, in fact, too low or limited for his ability or potential.   The adult who underestimates his ability and selects a course of study that is "safe" or "easy" but not challenging might feel just as frustrated as the per-

son who overestimates his ability and finds himself unable
to meet the requirements of the course of study. Either of
these unrealistic expectations can lead to frustration and
failure and the counselor must help the adult student in establishing realistic goals.

5. Irrelevancy and conflict. Another source of frustration for the adult is the inability to see any practical application of much of what he is required to learn. Adult
students tend to be practical and oriented toward their own
personal life experiences and/or future goals. It is often
difficult or impossible for them to relate information in
courses to anything that they have experienced or plan to
experience.

Attending school usually requires a large investment
in time and money for the adult and if he can see no practical use for that on which he is spending his time and
money, it can become a rather serious problem of motivation and a continuing irritation. The counselor can often
help in a situation of this type by pointing out to the student
possible associations between what they are learning and
their life experiences or goals. If this is difficult or impossible, as it sometimes will be, counseling may still serve a
very useful purpose by providing an opportunity for the student to express his frustration and anger. By getting things
"off his chest" the adult might be better able to cope with
his situation.

With a background of knowledge and experience, a
more firmly established life style, and sometimes strongly
held values, attitudes and beliefs, the adult may well run
into unsettling conflicts in the higher education setting.
Many of the ideas, attitudes and values discussed in the
classroom may be quite different from those which the adult
has developed over a long period of time. This calls for a
flexible, open approach on the part of the adult and it might
well be the task of the counselor to provide assistance in
this area.

6. Improper orientation to the higher education setting and process. One might advance the notion that students should be given three-quarter hour's credit in "academic problem solving" or something of the sort if they
have demonstrated the tenacity, adroitness and intelligence
required for successful completion of admission and registration procedures at most colleges and universities   For the
uninitiated and uninformed, this can be a harrowing experience.

For the adult, with all of the additional complications and
feelings of anxiety, it may well be enough to permanently
discourage him from embarking upon this new and rather
perilous experience.   In addition to being faced with a rather
confusing and complicated process, the adult student is often
hesitant in seeking help even if he knows where to find it.

A pre-admission or pre-registration group orientation
program might serve to inform the adult student, or potential student, of the mechanics involved in getting started in
the institution and individual counseling should always be
provided for those students who have special problems.

Relationship Between:
Educational Problems and Other Psychological Problems

At this point, it might be well to expand on the relationships and overlapping that exist between educational
problems as defined earlier and problems dealing with vocational choice, or those which might be identified as personal-
emotional in nature.   Educational problems may often involve
personal-emotional factors and/or concerns related to career
development.   As many critics contend, diagnostic classification of counseling problems is not without its weaknesses
and faults.   Anyone engaged in counseling realizes that the
identification, delineation and classification of counseling
problems is very difficult.

Bordin's discussion of the relation of psychological
counseling to other types of counseling points this out.   As
education has become more individualized in its treatment
of the student, educators have become more concerned with
special learning problems.   Consequently, provision is made
for special individualized help in improving such various
kinds of skills as reading, spelling, arithmetic, and well-
articulated speech, and in removing blocks to learning.
Specialists vary in the amount of attention they devote to
emotional factors in these difficulties.   There is relatively
little tendency to deny that these emotional factors are present; the big question is the extent to which they are the
roots of the difficulties and not simply their concomitants.
There seems to be no real need to choose between these
two views of the role of emotion and motivation.   One can
assume that persons with these learning difficulties will dis-
tribute themselves from the one extreme where the difficulty
arises primarily from mechanical sources or cognitive defects to the other extreme where the difficulty arises because

the particular skill has become invested with certain emotional conflicts of the individual.

To the extent that remedial work is aimed at rectify-
ing what must be defects in the learning sequences by which
a skill was acquired, remedial counseling moves away from
psychological counseling and is closer to teaching.   To the
extent that remedial work deals with emotional motivational
factors as sources of difficulty, it moves closer to psychological counseling.   When information is not enough, when the
student's use of the information reveals distorted thinking
and emotional conflict and the educational counselor begins
to deal with the emotional factors that influence the use of
information, then he begins to operate as a psychological
counselor. [7]

Fisher also points out

> ... there are numerous situations in which one's
> life functioning can be seriously impaired because
> of academic or scholastic difficulties.   Therefore,
> one must be prepared to find that a number of
> educational counseling cases may greatly resemble
> psychotherapy because of the central nature of
> education in self realization in today's society. [19]

Because of this, the counselor of adults must be
sensitive to those educational or academic problems which
are related to personal, emotional, vocational or other factors and must be prepared to deal with these as they come
out in the counseling process.   This calls for continuous
differential diagnosis or, if you prefer, formulating working
hypotheses on a moment-to-moment basis as the counseling
process continues in order for the counselor to determine
appropriate responses and treatment procedures.   A counsel-
or might very well in the course of a single counseling session begin with a practical problem of utilization of study
time and proceed into problems of concentration, disinterest
in school work, concern regarding appropriateness of a
major and perhaps finally end up in an involved emotional
discussion of parental pressure and problems in achieving
independence from the home.   It is obvious that the educational problem can develop into a much broader, more complex problem situation than the simple "I can't seem to organize my study time. "

The competent counselor must be willing and able to

use different approaches to assist the adult client in situations which go beyond the presented educational or academic problem. As Callis puts it

> ... the one-tool counselor must go. He is just as unscientific, unprofessional, unethical and immoral as the penicillin physician or the screwdriver mechanic. The only instance in which a counselor would be justified in restricting himself to one method would be for him to limit his practice to one type of inadequacy. [13]

Although the counselor must realize his professional limitations and be ready to utilize the services of other individuals or agencies when appropriate, the fact is that many counselors work in a setting which does not provide the luxury of selective clientele. That is, the counselor must work, not only in the educational problem area but also with problems dealing with career development and personal-emotional concerns. This ability to move with the client into those areas of concern to him, and to aid him in identifying, clarifying, and solving those problems requires skill in formulating hypotheses regarding the problem and determining appropriate treatment.

This concept of counseling may go beyond what some consider appropriate in a discussion of educational or academic problems. However, it makes little sense for a counselor to attempt to assist a student with problems related to study habits and skills and then, when these problems go beyond the academic area to include vocational-personal-emotional factors, to abruptly terminate the counseling contact in order to refer to a "vocational counselor" or "psychotherapist. "

There may be times, however, when the counselor will find that he is in a situation where a referral is appropriate.

The Problem of Referral

A crucial decision which must be made by the counselor of adults involves the question of whether to continue to work with a client or to refer him to an individual or agency which might be able to provide more competent or appropriate services for the client. Decisions regarding referral must take into account the following considerations:

(1) the professional competencies of the counselor; (2) available physical facilities and/or materials; (3) the defined areas of responsibility of the service or office in which the counselor is located; and (4) available referral services.

Some educational or academic counseling problems may be of such a nature that a rational, cognitive teaching approach might well suffice. In this case, a discussion of time utilization, note taking, various reading techniques, and the like might be all that is required. At other times, counseling might involve the discussion of attitudinal factors, motives, and values, in order to overcome the educational problem.

At times, the educational problem may be caused by dissatisfaction or confusion with vocational goals. That is, the client finds a course of study boring or too difficult and a reorientation toward different educational vocational goals will help to alleviate the problem.

At still other times, educational problems are symptomatic of more deeply rooted and chronic emotional difficulties. There may be times when the counselor, because of his background or the limitation of responsibility of the counseling service, feels it appropriate to refer to an agency or an individual prepared to undertake longer-term and more intensive psychotherapy. Unfortunately, there are no well-defined guidelines to determine at what point a referral should be made. Cases involving extreme anxiety, depression, hostility--especially if it might involve harm to the client himself or others, severe social inadequacies, drug use and abuse, and certain sexual concerns might all be considered for referral.

The decision regarding referral rests primarily with the counselor and he must be able to identify and make some determination regarding the seriousness of the problem in order to evaluate his own competence for treatment and to make some determination regarding responsibility of the office or service for treating such a problem. Although the counselor might be competent, the limitation of the work situation might dictate referral to another individual or agency.

Certain vocationally related problems requiring the use of standardized tests or other assessment procedures might also require a referral. Here, too, the professional

skill of the counselor is involved and, in addition, the availability of materials and proper physical facilities for testing
may determine whether a referral should be made.

The counselor working with adults primarily in the
area of educational or academic difficulties might be limited
in time, facilities, materials available and the defined responsibilities of the service so that certain vocational problems and/or personal emotional problems would best be referred to an agency, either on or off campus, which would
be more appropriate for the treatment of such problems.

The availability of appropriate referral services
might well be a problem.   One of the first tasks of a
counselor, when accepting a position, should be to identify
appropriate referral services on campus and in the community.   Contacts should be made and working relationships established between the counseling service and other psychological and psychiatric treatment facilities.   An important consideration should be the cost to the client.   Appropriate
services may be available without charge within the institution itself.   However, many institutions do not provide a
full range of psychological and psychiatric treatment facilities so that often referral to an off-campus agency or individual in private practice is necessary.   Community agencies often base fees on ability to pay and might be preferable
to the more costly private practitioner.

Effective referral to another service is a sensitive
and complex undertaking.   The client must have confidence
in the counselor resulting from the development of a good
relationship, and the approach and timing of the referral
must be given careful consideration by the counselor in
order to avoid a negative reaction from the client and the
possible rejection of not only the idea of referral but also
the counselor himself.   Braund suggests approaching the
subject of referral rather tentatively at first and then waiting until a later contact before becoming more specific.
He also points out that the client may be naive regarding
the type of assistance suggested and may need to be educated regarding the type of psychiatric or psychological
treatment recommended. [8]

Counseling for Educational Problems
(A Review of Some Recent Approaches)

Research evaluating counseling in terms of changes

in academic performance has yielded mixed results. This
brief review of research will concern itself primarily with
approaches that have reported positive results. Although
most of the research has not involved adult populations, it
would seem that many of the approaches described would be
applicable to adult students. In fact, due to the increased
maturity and motivation of the adult learner, it might be
speculated that counseling approaches would be even more
effective for the adult than for younger students.

Group Approaches

There has been a dramatic increase in the use of
group techniques in dealing with problems of educational or
academic nature in the past several years. Roth, Mauksch,
and Peiser provided group counseling to 174 failing students
at the Illinois Institute of Technology. Fifty-two subjects in
this population were selected at random for study and were
compared with 52 probationary noncounseled males who were
used as a comparison group. Results indicated that the
counseled group increased their grade point average significantly and that these changes held over time. [38]

A group of 19 college under-achievers were treated
with group therapy in a study reported by Thelen and Harris. This group was compared with 13 subjects who indicated interest in but did not receive group therapy. Results
indicated greater academic improvement and higher correla-
tions between adaptive or healthy personality variables and
academic improvement in the group receiving therapy. [40]

Abel reports a study of group counseling and academic
rehabilitation of probationary transfer students. Six group
meetings were held during a 9-week quarter. During these
meetings spontaneous discussions took place encompassing
various problems of campus life and emphasizing the norms
and expectancies in the academic and social areas. A two-
year follow up study of the counseled students in comparison
with a control group suggests that the group counseling was
an effective and efficient approach to helping probationary
transfer students to understand and perform satisfactorily
at their "new institution. "[1]

Chestnut compared "counselor-structured" and "group-
structured" counseling groups with a control group. The
groups were equal in ability and initial grade point averages.
Results indicated that the subjects in the "counselor-

structured" group had a significantly greater rate of change
in grade point average after counseling. It was concluded
that "counselor-structured" group experience can have both
an immediate and a delayed effect on academic achievement
with male college underachievers. [14]

Brown utilized upperclassmen as counselors and
found that counseled freshmen earned grades averaging one-
half letter-grade higher during their first semester of college. [10] Dickenson and Truax studied a group of underachieving college freshmen. They found that the 24 students who received group counseling showed a greater improvement in grade point average than 24 matched noncounseled control subjects. In addition, the counseled subjects who received the highest therapeutic conditions tended
to show the greatest improvement in grade point average. [16]

Gilbreath investigated the effects of two different
methods of group counseling on male, college underachievers.
He concluded that male underachievers with high dependency
needs improve their grade point average if they participate
in a high authority, leader-structured counseling program
and that more independent underachieving men improve in
grade point average in the low-authority, group-structured
counseling situation. This suggests that care should be
taken in evaluating the dependency needs of students in determining treatment procedures. [21]

Grenfell, although not reporting the results of research, does provide valuable observations in the area of
group counseling procedures for adult college students.
He offers a number of observations and suggestions about
group counseling with adults, many of which relate to the
educational-academic problem area. He emphasizes "here
and now" activities, planning for the future and ways the
college or university can be of assistance, and suggests
such activities as testing, pre-academic counseling or orientation to college and counseling programs for adults with
special needs and interests such as policemen, ministers,
women, businessmen, minority groups, and retirees.

Individual Counseling Approaches

Hendrix reports a study of the results of special advising on freshman achievement. A comparison was made
between the achievement of 20 college freshman students
with low predicted grade point averages (GPA) who received

special advising and a control group of 60 freshman students
with low predicted GPA who were advised by regular faculty
advisers.   The achievement of the experimental group was
significantly better than the control group on the basis of
several criteria. [24]

Rose identified 60 male freshman college students who
were considered potential dropouts.   One group of 30 was required to have 6 individual counseling interviews over a 12-
week period with a member of the counseling service staff.
The other group of 30 received no counseling.   Five students
from the control group dropped out while none from the counseled group withdrew from school. [37]

In a more recent study, Garner used both individual
counseling and environmental manipulation to help students
to cope with crisis situations during their first year in college.   The crisis intervention technique utilized was effective both in reducing the number of dropouts and improving
the academic performance of the experimental group. [20]

An interesting and relevant study is reported by Breen
on an active-directive counseling approach with adults.   This
article describes a very practical approach to the counseling
of adults and cites success in preventing 35 of 52 adult students from withdrawing from college. [9]

The University of Akron Testing and Counseling
Bureau conducted a counseling program for sophomore underachievers.   Of the students who were originally contacted by
letter, 25 began and 19 completed a program of pre-testing,
a minimum of three individual counseling sessions and post-
tests.   Of the 19 individuals completing all of the counseling
sessions, and the pre- and post-tests, 10 increased their
scores on the Brown-Holtzman Survey of Study Habits and
Attitudes.   The mean increase for the entire group was
34. 2 percentile points.   In addition, 13 of the 19 raised
their accumulative grade point average from the end of the
fall to the end of the winter quarter and 12 of the 19 raised
their GPA from the end of the winter quarter to the end of
the spring quarter.   The counseling sessions were approximately an hour in length and focused on those items on the
Brown-Holtzman which identified specific areas of weakness
in study habits and attitudes.

This brief review of research on counseling students
with educational problems suggests several trends: 1) an

increase in the use of group techniques which lends itself to coverage of common problems and issues; 2) the theme, repeated through a number of research programs, of establishing specific counseling goals and treatment procedures; and 3) the emphasis on behavioral techniques and directive-active "teaching" procedures.

The Learning and Study Skills Center

An approach which has been reported as achieving some success with undergraduate and graduate students and which should prove helpful to adults in alleviating educational problems is that of the learning and study skills laboratory or center.

One aspect of such a center is usually designed to increase reading speed and comprehension. At the University of Missouri, a formal course on reading speed and comprehension was moved from the Extension Division of the university to the new Learning Center of the Testing and Counseling Center. [28] Students requesting help with reading speed are referred to this formal course.

A second aspect of the University of Missouri program involved providing supplemental programmed texts for certain academic courses. In conjunction with the mathematics department, programmed texts in mathematics were reviewed and one such program selected for use in the center. In addition, a tutor from the mathematics department was assigned to the Learning Center to be available to help students in individual and group tutoring in connection with the use of the programmed materials. Acceptance of this program by students in mathematics was reported as immediate and enthusiastic.

In meeting the needs for an organized presentation of study-skill information, the Center developed a series of short courses in study skills. These courses consisted of eight one-hour sessions offered over a four-week period of time. Enrollment in each study-skills section was limited to 15 students.

Results of the study-skills courses were varied. As expected, the groups experienced an attrition rate of approximately 50 per cent. The counselors of the Testing and Counseling Service who conducted the groups suggest that such programs can be successful only if the material is

presented in an enthusiastic manner and if it contains information of practical value as perceived by group members.
Finally, it was observed that involvement of the group members is necessary in keeping attrition down and in producing
a meaningful experience for the student.

Highline Community College in Midway, Washington,
presents a progress report on a model Learning Skills
Laboratory. [25]   The laboratory was designed to provide
self-instructional materials and machine aids which would
enable students to devise their own individualized remedial
programs.   In addition, short-term, small-group workshops
focusing on listening skills, techniques of note-taking, critical reading, and taking tests are open to all students on
a voluntary basis.

A pre-testing program involving the Wechsler Adult
Intelligence Scale, the Self-Concept Scale, and diagnostic
tests in certain academic areas, provide a base line from
which students chart their own progress.   The program is
designed to be noncompetitive, nonpunitive and completely
voluntary with no registration fees or grades involved.

The atmosphere in the laboratory is described as
casual with free coffee and smoking permitted.   Private,
semi-private, and open study areas are available at the
students' option.   The staff consists of visiting scholars
provided by a U. S. Office of Education grant, the project
director who is also the director of counseling for the college, and members of the college counseling staff and
secretarial and technical assistants.

The report evaluated the experience of approximately
100 students who worked on individual skill development over
a period of two years and approximately 170 others attending the workshop sessions.   An evaluation of the program
noted the following factors:

     1.   Many of the students who used the self-in-
structional materials were highly motivated,
older, married men with a large percentage
returning veterans.

     2.   Counselors aided many students in their initial
efforts.

     3.   Over half of the participants were deficient in

several skill areas and most worked on all areas.

4. As they experienced success, students were able to work more on their own, and greater self-respect and self-confidence developed in those who persisted.

5. A correlation of .40 was found between hours spent in lab work and change in grades.

6. More realistic assessment of abilities and achievement resulted in some students continuing their educational program while others decided to terminate their programs. However, either decision was seen as representing "growth."

Summary

As heterogeneous as the typical entering freshman class of a college or university may be, it is unlikely that it approaches the diversity in abilities, interests, experiences, and problems of a group of adults entering college for the first time. Because of this diversity and often the responsibilities of family and job, the adult student is likely to have greater need for counseling than the younger college student. Although the adult may have other problems which might be more appropriately classified as personal-emotional, or vocational rather than educational, if he is helped to achieve success in the classroom and is making progress toward an appropriate educational goal, many of the other problems will be either eliminated altogether or minimized to such an extent that they become relatively unimportant.

References

1. Abel, W. H., "Group Counseling and Academic Rehabilitation of Probationary Transfer Students," Journal of College Student Personnel, 1967, vol. 8, pp. 185-188.

2. Albert, G., "A Survey of Counseling Facilities," Personnel and Guidance Journal, 1968, vol. 46, pp. 540-543.

3.   Anderson, W. , "Services Offered by College Counseling
     Centers", Journal of Counseling Psychology, 1970,
     vol. 17, pp. 380-382.

4.   Apostal, R. A. and Miller, J. G. , "A Manual for the
     Use of a Set of Diagnostic Categories, " Columbia:
     University of Missouri Testing and Counseling Serv-
     ice Report No. 21, 1959 (Mimeo).

5.   Berezin, Annabel G. , "The Development and Use of a
     System of Diagnostic Categories in Counseling. "
     Unpublished doctoral dissertation, University of
     Missouri, 1957.

6.   Bordin, E. S. , "Diagnosis in Counseling and Psycho-
     therapy. " Educational Psychological Measurement,
     1946, vol. 6, pp. 169-184.

7.   Bordin, E. S. , Psychological Counseling. New York:
     Appleton Century Crofts, 1968, pp. 21-11.

8.   Braund, J. C. , "The General Counselor and Counsel-
     ing" in M. L. Farmer, ed. , Student Personnel
     Services for Adults in Higher Education, Metuchen,
     N. J. : Scarecrow Press, 1967 pp. 149-163.

9.   Breen, G. J. , "Active-Directive Counseling in an
     Adult Education Setting, " Journal of College Student
     Personnel, 1970, vol. 11, pp. 279-283.

10. Brown, W. F. , "Student to Student Counseling for
     Academic Adjustment, " Personnel and Guidance
     Journal, 1965, vol. 43, pp. 811-817.

11. Byrne, R. H. , "Proposed Revisions of the Bordin-
     Pepinsky Diagnostic Constructs, " Journal of Counsel-
     ing Psychology, 1958, vol. 5, pp. 184-188.

12. Callis, R. , "Diagnostic Classification as a Research
     Tool, " Journal of Counseling Psychology, 1965, vol.
     12, pp. 238-243.

13. Callis, R. , "Toward an Integrated Theory of Counsel-
     ing, " Journal of College Student Personnel, 1960,
     vol. 1, pp. 2-9.

14. Chestnut, W. J. , "The Effects of Structured and Un-

structured Group Counseling on Male College Students' Underachievement, " Journal of Counseling Psychology, 1965, vol. 12, pp. 388-398.

15. Clark, D. D. , "Characteristics of Counseling Centers in Large Universities, " Personnel and Guidance Journal, 1966, vol. 44, pp. 817-823.

16. Dickenson, W. A. and Truax, C. B. , "Group Counseling with College Underachievers, " Personnel and Guidance Journal, 1966, vol. 45, pp. 243-247.

17. English, H. B. and English A. , A Comprehensive Dictionary of Psychological and Psychoanalytical Terms, New York: David McKay, 1968.

18. Farmer, M. L. (Ed.) Student Personnel Services for Adults in Higher Education, Metuchen, N. J. : Scarecrow Press, 1967.

19. Fisher, J. A. , "Educational Counseling for Adults, " in C. H. Thompson, ed. , Counseling Adults: Contemporary Dimension, A Report of Commission XIII, Student Personnel Services for Adults in Higher Education, American College Personnel Association, Las Vegas, Nevada, 1969.

20. Garner, W. C. , "The Crisis Intervention Technique with Potential College Dropouts, " Personnel and Guidance Journal, 1970, vol. 48, pp. 552-560.

21. Gilbreath, S. H. , "Group Counseling Dependence and College Male Underachievement, " Journal of Counseling Psychology, 1967, vol. 14 pp. 449-453.

22. Goodstein, L. D. , "Five-Year Follow-up of Counseling Effectiveness with Probationary College Students, " Journal of Counseling Psychology, 1967, vol. 14, pp. 436-439.

23. Grenfell, J. E. , "Group Counseling for Adult College Students, " in: C. H. Thompson, ed. , Counseling Adults: Contemporary Dimension, A Report of Commission XIII, Student Personnel Services for Adults in Higher Education, American College Personnel Association, Las Vegas, Nevada, 1969.

24.   Hendrix, O. R., "The Effect of Special Advising on
      Achievement of Freshmen With Low Predicted Grades,"
      Personnel and Guidance Journal, 1965, vol. 44, pp.
      185-188.

25.   Highline Community College, Student Personnel Services
      Counseling Center, Progress Report, May 1969.

26.   Hill, A. H. and Grieneeks, L., "An Evaluation of
      Academic Counseling of Under and Over-Achievers,"
      Journal of Counseling Psychology, 1966, vol. 13,
      pp. 325-328.

27.   Island, D. D., "Counseling Students with Special Prob-
      lems," Review of Educational Research, 1969, vol.
      39, pp. 239-250.

28.   Johnston, J. and Irvin J., Operations: Learning Cen-
      ter, University of Missouri, "Testing and Counseling
      Service Report No. 1" 21, (Mimeo).

29.   Klein, P. E. and Moffit, R. E., Counseling Techniques
      in Adult Education, McGraw-Hill, New York, 1946.

30.   Kramer, H. C., "Effects of Conditioning Several Re-
      sponses in a Group Setting," Journal of Counseling
      Psychology, 1968, vol. 15, pp. 58-62.

31.   New England Board of Higher Education and the Center
      for the Study of Liberal Education for Adults at
      Boston University: Proceedings of the Conference
      on the Training of Counselors for Adults, Chatham,
      Mass., May 1965, p. 169.

32.   Nugent, F. A. and Pareis, E. N., "Survey of Present
      Policies and Practices in College Counseling Centers
      in the United States of America," Journal of Counsel-
      ing Psychology, 1968, vol. 15, pp. 94-97.

33.   Oetting, E. R., "Problems and Issues in the Adminis-
      tration of College and Community Counseling Services,"
      (Final Report to United States Office of Education,
      Grant No. OE-5-10-302) Fort Collins: Colorado
      State University, 1967.

34. Palais, E. S., "What is Evening Student Personnel?," in: M. L. Farmer, ed., Student Personnel Services for Adults in Higher Education, Metuchen, N. J.: Scarecrow Press, 1967, pp. 40-64.

35. Pepinsky, H. B., "The Selection and Uses of Diagnostic Categories in Clinical Counseling," Applied Psychology Monographs, 1948, p. 15.

36. Rackham, E. N., Student Personnel Services Inventory, Kent, Ohio: 1963.

37. Rose, Harriet A., "Prediction and Prevention of Freshman Attrition," Journal of Counseling Psychology, 1965, vol. 12, pp. 399-403.

38. Roth, R. M., Mauksch, H. O., and Peiser, K., "The Nonachievement Syndrome, Group Therapy and Achievement Change," Personnel and Guidance Journal, 1967, vol. 5, pp. 189-195.

39. Sloan, T. J. and Pierce-Jones, J., "The Bordin-Pepinsky Diagnostic Categories: Counselor Agreement and MMPI Comparisons," Journal of Counseling Psychology, 1958, pp. 189-195.

40. Thelan, J. H. and Harris, C. S., "Personality of College Underachievers Who Improve with Group Psychotherapy," Personnel and Guidance Journal, 1968, vol. 46, pp. 561-566.

41. Weiner, I. B., "The Role of Diagnosis in a University Counseling Center," Journal of Counseling Psychology, 1959, vol. 6, pp. 110-115.

42. Williamson, E. G. and Darley, J. G., Student Personnel Work, New York: McGraw-Hill, 1937.

Chapter IV

VOCATIONAL COUNSELING FOR THE ADULT STUDENT
IN HIGHER EDUCATION

By Goldie Ruth Kaback

Introduction

Time was when students came to college or the university for an education: to acquire knowledge and wisdom, to be steeped in the classics, and to ponder the variegated paths of truth. Today, learning for learning's sake is no longer in vogue. Education, particularly for those over 30, now usually means a better job, more income, increased leisure; sometimes it means meeting the right people and assuring one's future.

While education may be expressed in terms of dollars and cents, it is also a nexus with one's efforts to best the Computer Age. Estimates with regard to computor efficiency suggest that computors now can do whatever the average high school graduate can do, and in 50 years, computors well may replace those with average to high-average intellectual competency. This means that lower and middle management, clerical, sales, and service workers will ultimately find themselves in the same surplus category that unskilled labor finds itself today. Can it be that the adult student hears the message and searches, through education, for ways to cope with the coming Computor Age? Does he seek vocational counseling to better his economic station in life? What does vocational counseling mean to him? What does he expect from the vocational counselor? How might a vocational counselor help him to prepare for a world of work that is as yet unnamed and technically unknown?

Principles of Vocational Counseling

The first description of vocational counseling in this country is ascribed to Frank Parsons, who in 1909 wrote that vocational counseling included:

> ... a clear understanding of yourself, your apti-
> tudes, your abilities, interests, ambitions, re-
> sources, limitations and their causes; a knowledge
> of the requirements and conditions of success, ad-
> vantages, compensations, opportunities and pros-
> pects in different lines of work, and true reason-
> ing on the relations of these two groups of facts. [31]

Other definitions that have since been offered may be more
detailed and include more emphasis on the inter-personal
relationships between counselor and counselee but the basic
principles for vocational counseling first enunciated in Par-
son's Choosing a Vocation still hold. [34, 45, 47, 55, 56, 57]

For adult students in higher education, the concept
of vocational counseling includes the process of helping an
individual to understand the variety of influences in his life
that have led him to his present work and study role; to
re-evaluate his work role in light of his more mature,
realistic appreciation of his potentialities against the opportunities now available to him in a demanding, complex society; and to derive maximum personal satisfaction from his
efforts. [45]

Not long ago, vocational counseling was elicited, tests
were administered, job requirements were checked by the
counselor and then, after matching job requirements with an
estimate of the counselee's assets and limitations, the
counselee was advised to consider indicated occupations.
It was assumed that dissatisfaction with one's work-role
was due solely to a lack of information about one's self
and the world of work. [45]

A more recent influence on the vocational counseling
process has been Roger's nondirective or client-centered
approach. Here the emphasis is primarily on attitudes and
feelings rather than on so-called objective facts. The client
is helped to explore his attitudes and feelings, and to develop self-understanding and self-acceptance without the benefit of tests and educational and vocational information. [38, 39]

The confusion resulting from the use of either the inventory method of test results and information-giving, or the
method of exploring attitudes and feelings without the use of
tests and occupational information, has been a source of
conflict for the counselor who works primarily with adults.
On the one hand, the counselor has been trained to use

tests and occupational information. On the other hand, he
recognizes the importance of emotional influences and the
adult's mature concept of self as a determinant in the formu-
lation of occupational decisions. In order to resolve the
problem, those counselors who have felt more comfortable
with tests and information-giving continue to do so, reason-
ing that client-centered counseling and self-concept ideologies
do not necessarily apply to vocational counseling with adults.

Those, however, who have studied this pertinent situation and have made serious attempts to understand the client-
centered approach are convinced that the basic principles of
counseling with the client as the core are as applicable to
vocational counseling as they are to personal counseling. [20, 21, 22, 23, 24, 25, 34]

According to Patterson, they feel "... the essence of
counseling is the relationship. It is not the use of the interview, of tests, of specific techniques, or the surroundings
which constitute counseling."[34]

Patterson goes on to stress the in-counseling and the
fact that it is the counselor who assists the client to change
and to become competent to make choices so that he can resolve his problems and develop a responsible independence
which make him a better member of society. This description of counseling in no way prevents the counselor from
using tests and occupational information where needed. There
need be no conflict between client-centered counseling and
educational and vocational counseling with adults. Tests and
occupational information are appropriate where they are needed and where they are useful to help a client solve a problem and make a decision. [39]

The techniques used for personal counseling can be
adapted to vocational counseling. One cannot separate a
counselee's vocational needs from his attitudes, feelings and
general personal adjustment. There are very few problems
that are solely vocational in nature. Content material from
counseling sessions with adults include feelings about self,
employer, and family, although the initial reason for scheduling the interview might well have been a need for vocational
counseling. If one continues to interview the adult, he will
reveal vocational and avocational interests: the kind of person he would prefer to work with and why; his vocational
objectives in light of his abilities, interests, and hobbies;
and the barriers or conflicts that prevent the fulfillment of

his vocational objectives.   The adult's associations evoked
during the interview relate not only to vocations but also to
personal involvement and personal needs which may sometimes have little to do with test results and occupational
information.

There are those who speak of vocational counseling
as a distinct area of student personnel work where "normal"
individuals (whatever "normal" means) come only for assistance with vocational decisions.   It may be that there are
such people whose emotional concerns are of secondary importance compared to their occupational problems, but unfortunately, this type of "normal" individual is a rarity.
The vocational counselor is interested in the whole person;
his present work situation; his vocational aspirations and
the personality dynamics of conflict and frustration which
prevent him from achieving maximum satisfaction in his
personal life and vocational role. [36, 47]

There is no dichotomy between the personal self and
the vocational self.   Numerous studies have indicated that
those who are least able to experience gratification in employment are also more likely to face difficulties in achieving a satisfactory state in their personal lives.   Those who
are above average in job satisfaction are happier and better
adjusted people.   The lower the level of job satisfaction, the
greater the mental health risk. [11, 12, 26, 27, 41, 53]

Vocational counseling with adults means a deep, sensitive appreciation of the adult and his problems, the possible
utilization of tests and occupational information where and
when needed, an understanding of the socio-economic influences within the society in which the adult lives, and an
awareness of the impact of these influences on his life and
inter-personal relationships.   The adult's socio-economic
situation may call for an immediate and specific vocational
decision and it may be the counselor's job to help the adult
reach that decision in light of certain unpredictable and un-
foreseen circumstances.   The counselor, however, always
leaves the door open so that the adult may return when such
circumstances have changed.

Vocational counseling with adults calls for an understanding of the effects of job choice on family responsibilities which the adult has undertaken.   Having a wife and
several children dependent on one's earnings might well
preclude immediate try-outs in new vocational areas, no

matter what one's interests, abilities and potentialities may
be.   Under these conditions, vocational counseling might become family counseling.   This is not to say "once a teacher,
always a teacher" or "once a plumber, always a plumber. "
It does suggest, however, a realistic awareness of the many
many issues that must be considered in the realm of vocational counseling with adults.   Following a sequence of suggested course credits, for example, may open or close vocational doors to the adult.   Terminal education in a junior
college (unless the college has a transfer program) may
make it more difficult for the adult to continue on toward a
baccalaureate degree which is a requirement for many vocational areas.   Immersed in courses in which one is primarily
concerned without regard to other programs of study designed
to develop an individual into a well-rounded and intelligent
person may also limit the adult's success in his chosen vocational field.   More than one successful business or professional man has been heard to say, "I miss the background
in art and literature and music; my concentration was solely
in economics, or the sciences, or business administration;
now I meet men in my kind of work who are as much at
home in the arts as they are in business or in the professions and I feel inadequate. "   The excitement and hopefulness
of all this is that many of these same men are now returning
to evening colleges in search of an intellectual stimulation
that will enrich their everyday working lives.

        Vocational decisions for the adult become less and
less reversible as he grows older, for he has already invested much time and energy and thought in his decisions.
Counseling in this area, therefore, brings with it the need
to recognize the effect of technological and scientific changes
in the adult's work role--how he evaluates himself as he is
threatened by the introduction of new machines and bright,
young men who appear to have all the answers.   Finally,
counseling the adult also includes ways of helping him to
modify his work load as he begins to feel the effects of
his years, and suddenly, albeit subtly, the work-role is no
longer as important as the "golden years" that lie ahead.

                The Role of the Vocational Counselor

        It takes courage for a mature adult to seek advice
from another adult.   As courageous as he may appear to
be, the adult fears change and the delving into his dreams
and vocational aspirations.   The vocational counselor's role

then becomes one of helping the adult to perceive the basis
for his fears and the very real obstructions which deter or
promote the actualization of his plans. The counselor knows
that an adult's career choice may have a tremendous influence on his life. It may determine his social class, his
dress, his hobbies, his goals and values, his politics, the
geographic locale of his home, his physical and mental
health, and his opinions and attitudes toward life itself. [37, 38]

Although a vocational counselor may anticipate the effects of various vocational controls on an adult's self-system, it is the adult himself who ultimately determines the
direction of his vocational decision with such assistance as
he is willing and able to accept from the counselor. The
counselor must, in turn, respect the adult's plan even though
it differs from his own.

Any individual in a democratic society and a democratic vocational counseling setting cannot arbitrarily be assigned
to a vocation by a counselor despite the result of aptitude
tests and cues from interest inventories. The individual has
the freedom to choose his own vocation, although the limitations imposed on him by a changing, scientific society and
the unique characteristics of his own personality are important considerations. Moreover, the vocational counselor
must be perceptive of the ties that exist between the adult's
underlying drives, motives and vocational goals. The need
to be accepted and approved by others and to find a vocation suitable for one's social class (the social conformity
drive), may well be the reasons for adult's vocational goals.
The need to meet and to work with others, yet to maintain
an impersonal aloofness might be the reason for a second
adult's vocational choice. The need for freedom to be one's
own boss (which may be related to a strict authoritarian
home, according to psychoanalytic theory) may yet be another
reason. The need for economic security--a job with tenure,
a pension, and defined working conditions--and a need for
power control or social admiration and attention-getting may
underline the vocational goals of still other adults. [31]

The vocational counselor then requires a knowledge
about the whole self-system of the person; his decision-
making process, the values and goals to which he subscribes,
his degree of self-awareness with respect to limitations and
assets, as well as his entire philosophy of life. An adult's
interest in preparing for a career or entering a specific
occupation or advancing in it is not enough. The vocational

counselor must find out how the adult feels about himself.
How realistic are his appraisals of his abilities in relation
to job opportunities and how does he view his responsibilities
to others who may be dependent upon him? Certainly, it is
not as easy for an adult with dependents as it might be for a
younger person to leave a job today in order to take his
chances on getting a better one tomorrow.   The vocational
counselor, therefore, must take into consideration the economic status of the adult and his sense of responsibility for
others; his strength to withstand failures and his ability to
weather risks.

It may sometimes be necessary to invite the wife of
the adult student into the vocational counseling process in
order to determine her views with respect to new vocational
considerations.   An adult student's enthusiasm for a new vocational venture does not preclude conflict and frustration
that may result from a wife's inability to pay the butcher,
the baker and the candlestick maker.

Exploration with respect to dislike or dissatisfaction
with the old vocation is certainly indicated.   The vocational
counselor's appraisal of the adult's feelings related to outcomes is certainly most important in helping him to chart a
vocational future.   The adult's use of rationalization, reac-
tion-formation, identification and the like should offer important signals to the counselor regarding an adult's real
need for vocational change.

The Adult Student's Expectations From
Vocational Counseling

The adult in higher education is certainly more vocationally mature than the average college student.   He has
already been initiated into the world of work and he knows
its demands, its opportunities, its conflicts, and its failures
and successes.   His own particular job may call for more
originality and initiative than he has to offer or he may have
more originality than the present job demands.   He may
know what he wants to achieve but be ill-informed with respect to the proper vocational outlets for his needs.   He
may wish to narrow a wide range of vocational interests or
simply come in to discuss the pros and cons of a vocational
decision already made.   He may want assistance in order
to understand himself better in relation to his projected vocational goals. [45, 46] He may be involved in an examination
of personal values and how these may be affected by a new

job choice.   The academic setting may have triggered a self-concept formerly held but now long dormant under the impact of a job situation that has held few satisfactions in its daily demands.

Although cues with regard to any of the dimensions indicated will be picked up by the trained, perceptive vocational counselor, he must try to understand the real reasons that brought the adult into the counseling situation and what the adult expects from the counseling interaction.

First and foremost, the adult expects to be accepted as an equal.   He resents the dichotomy of informed counselor and uninformed counselee.   He wants to be respected for what he knows.   He also expects to be helped to make a decision but not to have decisions made for him.   While he may welcome assistance with regard to specific programs of study which might help to prepare him for his future vocational role, he also wants the freedom to rearrange those programs of study in light of his own immediate needs. [11]

The adult student in higher education is usually employed.   He has, however, become aware of the growing disruptions in the economy and he wishes to prepare himself for the new economic status.   Usually he does not need job placement.   A work-role for the average adult is not a new experience.   Because of his familiarity with the issues and demands of a work-oriented society, he turns to vocational counseling in the hope that the counseling interaction will somehow help him to open up locked doors, and thus provide him with greater satisfaction from work than he is currently experiencing. [37]   He expects professional assistance with respect to career planning, that is, which sequence of occupations, jobs and positions must he prepare for during the course of his working life that will yield those values which he now deems important for himself. [41, 53]   The counselor, however, must also be alert to the fact that while the adult may have the opportunity to change to a job which would be more satisfying, he may not always be ready for that change. [14]

While the adult may be more interested in career planning than in jobs per se, he does expect that the vocational counselor will have some knowledge of the economy with respect to rising or declining occupations.   He expects the vocational counselor to be informed with regard to on-the-job training facilities and the specific employers who

are interested in financing a college for their employees.
He further expects the counselor to know something about
union membership, fringe benefits in a variety of industries
and employment trends on a local and national level.

The adult student assumes that the vocational counsel-
or will have more vocational information than he has, will
know more about the socio-economic trends of the economy
than he knows, and may even know more about him as a
person than he knows about himself. [14, 43, 44, 45]

The need for vocational change is not always of the
adult's own choosing. It is well known that the average
person today will probably need to consider and to enter
four or more different vocations and/or fields during his
lifetime because of the rapid technological and scientific
changes in our society. It is expected that the vocational
counselor, if he is to meet the adult's expectations, will be
informed with respect to the effects of automation on jobs;
what new occupations are appearing; in what way the manpower needs of a particular community are related to the
manpower needs of the nation. The counselor is expected
to know whether there is a down-grading of skills formerly
held in high respect; whether many jobs today warrant the
higher levels of education and experience indicated; whether
the human being is becoming a useless organism to be tolera-
ted by the machine.

The adult expects the vocational counselor to be aware
of the effects of the educational revolution now taking place
in the schools and colleges and to have an informed opinion
as to whether society will continue to cling to rather well-
defined middle-class values or whether it will have to modify
and revise such values in light of increasing demands from
those under 30. The vocational counselor will have to be
fortified with knowledge about an ever-increasing labor force
of professionals, technicians, managers, and officials with
but a small underpinning of service workers and farmers.
Many of the adults who come to the vocational counselor
need updating, retraining or training for a new field of
work because their old jobs are being phased out. Many
of the adults come because they have begun to recognize
within themselves new intellectual and emotional strengths
which can, in large measure, only be actualized through new
vocational endeavors guided by an understanding, well-informed vocational counselor.

While it can generally be inferred that reference to the adult student in higher education includes both men and women, perhaps a special note should be made with respect to the woman student who has returned to further her education. More often than not, she has the same vocational needs and drives for social and monetary positions as does the male adult student. She has begun to play a very important role in the national labor force. She is employed in every occupation and profession listed in the decennial census. (She has even invaded that highly prized male sanctum-sanctorum, horse racing.) Federal legislation now assures her an equal opportunity and equal pay in the economy. Financial assistance for vocational training, advanced courses and higher education are becoming increasingly available to her. At the present time, nearly half the women in the population between the ages of 18 and 65 are in the labor force and the percentage continues to rise rapidly. [52, 16] Her expectations from vocational counseling are no different from those of her male counterpart.

When the adult woman comes to the counselor for vocational counseling, she has already gone beyond her earlier dreams of a romantic image of life--school, marriage, a family, and a happy life ever after. She now knows that a more accurate life pattern of the modern woman includes school, work, and/or marriage which entails rearing a family while continuing to work either by choice or necessity or a return to work when the youngest child is in school. The increase in teenage marriages means that about half of today's women are married by the age of 21; they have their last child at about the age of 30. By the time the youngest child is in school, a mother may have 30 to 35 more years of active life before her. [52]

Economic projections through the 1980's indicate that women and youth will provide the largest source of new entrants into the labor force. About 29 million women, 16 years of age and over, are in the labor force; more than one out of every three workers is a woman; almost three out of five women workers are married (58 per cent); 21 per cent are single; 21 percent are widowed, divorced or separated and about 2.7 million women workers are heads of their families. [28]

This quiet revolution in the life pattern of American women presents a special challenge to the vocational counselor. Many have returned and many more will continue to

return to school to pick up where they have left off.   They
will expect the vocational counselor to assist them with personal and vocational decisions.

It is only recently that men in the labor force have
caught up with women in terms of education, according to
the National Consumer Finance Association.   The median
level for both is 12. 4 years of schooling.   In 1940, the
first year for which figures are available, the median level
for men in the labor force was 8. 6 years of school, while
for women, it was 11 years.   By 1952, men were narrowing
the gap with 10. 6 years, against 12 years for women.

> The factors that led to 1970's 12. 4 figure, which
> includes several months beyond high school, are
> increasing affluence, changing attitudes and tech-
> nological evolution that have created a demand for
> more educated workers.   These same factors
> also helped bring more women into the labor force.
> Between 1968 and 1970, women accounted for 57
> per cent or a 3. 9 million net increase in the labor
> force, or roughly 2. 2 million.   Of these, 1. 8 mil-
> lion were married.   Employment rates for women
> with less than 12 years of schooling have been low
> and remained so according to the report, but em-
> ployment rates for those with more than 12 years
> of education have climbed.   High school graduates
> in major occupational classifications break down
> as follows: white collar, 32. 1 million of the 37. 3
> million workers, or 86 per cent, up from 76 per
> cent in 1959; blue collar, 12. 5 million of the 26. 7
> million workers, or 47 per cent, up from 32 per
> cent in 1959; service occupations, 4. 2 million of
> the 8. 9 million, or 47 per cent, up from 32 per
> cent in 1959; farm jobs, 1 million of the 2. 8 mil-
> lion, or 36 per cent, up from 24 per cent in
> 1959. [59]

Job Satisfaction Through Vocational Counseling

The adult student's expectation from vocational counseling also includes assistance with planning for either the
professions or for those upper-level business positions that
will presumably yield greater personal satisfaction than
they now derive from their present work roles.

The Manpower Report of 1968 states that:

The higher an individual's position in the occupational hierarchy, the more likely he is to experience satisfaction in his employment .... [T]he
findings of job satisfaction studies have been consistent and generally unequivocal. Satisfaction is
greater among white-collar than blue-collar workers as a whole, and typically is found to be highest among professionals and businessmen and lowest among unskilled laborers. [28]

Gurin and his associates in their book Americans View
Their Mental Health found, for example, that the highest
proportion, 42 per cent of very satisfied workers, was in
the professional-technical classification and the lowest, 13
per cent, in the unskilled laborer group. The clerical and
the sales workers surveyed in the study expressed somewhat
less satisfaction with their employment than did semi-skilled
manual workers. A relatively high level of satisfaction was
expressed by farmers despite the downward trends of agri-
cultural employment. [18] In this connection, it might be well
to note that selective factors are possibly at work since
many of the people most dissatisfied with farming are likely
to have migrated to urban areas and those who remain, or
are drawn to farming, are probably those to whom the general life style of farming is more appealing than the com-
plexities of urban life.

The relative importance of the different factors in
job satisfaction or dissatisfaction is found to vary by occupational groups. What an individual perceives as satisfying
or dissatisfying is necessarily determined by his own values,
needs, motives and expectations, as well as by the objective
features of his present working environment. Different
groups may have quite different reactions to the same set
of job circumstances.

Thus, Centers and Bugental, in their recent study of
work motivations of members of an urban population, found
that, by and large, workers in white-collar categories attached greater significance to the intrinsic factors related
to the work itself, that it be interesting and make satisfying
use of the worker's skills and talents, while the blue-collar
workers placed comparatively greater stress on factors per-
taining to the context in which the work was performed:
the extrinsic factors of pay; job security, and co-workers. [5]
However, it should be noted that a job which calls for the
exercise of considerable skill or talent including higher

education is also more likely to provide higher wages which
is generally a good measure of job security and more than
minimally adequate working conditions.

Do nonwork activities provide greater satisfaction
than work activities? Does going to school provide greater
satisfaction for the adult student than his daily work situation? There are very few studies in this regard, but Friedlander in 1966 found that among government workers, at
least, work is the pivot around which their other activities
are planned. On the average, both blue- and white-collar
respondents considered their jobs far more important to
feelings of satisfaction or dissatisfaction than recreation,
education or church. [10]

While the counselor might well consider the goal of
job-satisfaction as but one of the more important aspects of
the vocational counseling process, and the adult student's
educational preparation as a major phase toward his future
vocational career, the counselor must not lose sight of the
fact that education can, at its best, transcend preparation
for work by unveiling to the adult the deeper intellectual
and emotional experiences that exist outside of a work situation. [11, 35] For in the words of Cicero, "Nor is it the body
only that must be supported, but still more the intellect and
the soul, for they are like lamps--unless you feed them with
oil, they go out. "

References

1.   Bare, Carole E. , "Personality and Self-Concept Cor-
       relates of Occupational Aspirations, " Vocational
       Guidance Quarterly, June 1970, pp. 297-305.

2.   Beilin, H. , "The Application of General Developmental
       Principles to the Vocational Area, " Journal of
       Counseling Psychology, 1955, vol. 2, pp. 53-57.

3.   Blauner, R. , "Work Satisfaction and Industrial Trends
       in Modern Society, " in: Galenson, W. , and Lipset,
       S. M. , eds. , Labor and Trade Unionism, New York:
       Wiley, 1960, pp. 339-360.

4.   Borow, H. , "An Integral Overview of Occupational
       Theory and Research, " in: Man in a World at Work,
       Boston: Houghton Mifflin, 1964.

5. Centers, R. and Bugental, Daphne E. , "Intrinsic and
    Extrinsic Job Motivation among Different Segments
    of the Working Population, " Journal of Applied
    Psychology, June 1966, pp. 193-197.

6. Clark, J. V. , "Motivation in Work Groups, a Tenta-
    tive View, " Human Organization, 1960-1961, vol.
    19, pp. 199-208.

7. Drucker, P. F. , "The Psychology of Managing Manage-
    ment, " Psychology Today, March 1968, vol. 1, pp.
    62-66.

8. Drucker, P. F. , "America's Next Twenty Years: The
    Promise of Automation, " Harper's Magazine, April
    1955, pp. 41-47; May 1955, pp. 39-44.

9. Freedman, Marcia K. , The Process of Work Establish-
    ment, New York: Columbia University Press, 1966.

10. Friedlander, F. , "Importance of Work Versus Non-Work
    among Socially and Occupationally Stratified Groups, "
    Journal of Applied Psychology, December 1966, pp.
    437-441.

11. Gardner, J. W. , Excellence: Can We Be Excellent and
    Equal, Too?, New York: Harper and Row, 1961.

12. Gardner, J. W. , Self-Renewal: The Individual and the
    Innovative Society, New York: Harper and Row,
    1964.

13. Gellman, W. , "Government and Community Settings
    for Vocational Guidance, " in: Borow, H. , ed. ,
    Man in a World at Work, Boston: Houghton Mifflin,
    1964.

14. Ginzberg, E. , et al. , Occupational Choice, New York:
    Columbia University Press, 1951.

15. Ginzberg, E. , "Guidance--Limited or Unlimited, "
    Personnel and Guidance Journal, 1960, vol. 38,
    pp. 707-712.

16. Ginzberg, E. , Life Styles of Educated Women, New
    York: Columbia University Press, 1966.

17. Gross, E. , Work and Society, New York: Thomas Y.
    Crowell, 1958.

18. Gurin, G. , Veroff, J. and Feld, Sheila, Americans
    View Their Mental Health, New York: Basic Books,
    1960.

19. Holland, J. L. , "A Theory of Vocational Choice, "
    Journal of Counseling Psychology, 1959, vol. 6,
    pp. 35-45.

20. Kaback, Goldie R. , "The Training of Student Personnel
    Workers for Evening Colleges, " Evening Student
    Personnel Association Convention Proceedings, 1963,
    pp. 30-39.

21. Kaback, Goldie R. , "The Selection and Preparation of
    Student Personnel Workers for Adults in Evening
    Colleges, " in: M. L. Farmer, ed. , Student Per-
    sonnel Services for Adults in Higher Education,
    Metuchen, N. J. ; Scarecrow Press, 1967, pp. 164-
    180.

22. Kaback, Goldie R. , "Implications for Counseling the
    Adult, " American College Personnel Association:
    Proceedings of a Pre-Convention workshop, Counsel-
    ing the Adult Student, a report of Commission XIII,
    1967, pp. 12-20.

23. Kaback, Goldie R. , "The Selection and Training of
    Student Personnel Workers for Adults in Institutions
    of Higher Learning, " American College Personnel
    Association: Proceedings of a Pre-Convention work-
    shop, Counseling the Adult Student, a report of Com-
    mission XIII, 1967, pp. 28-38.

24. Kaback, Goldie R. , "Educating and Motivating Individuals
    for the Profession: Student Personnel Work with
    Adults, " Evening Student Personnel Association Fifth
    Annual Convention Proceedings, 1967, pp. 71-78.

25. Kaback, Goldie R. , "Counseling: The Counselor Vis-a-
    Vis the Counselee, " American College Personnel
    Association: Proceedings of a Pre-Convention work-
    shop, College Personnel Services for the Adult, a
    report of Commission XIII, 1968, pp. 27-34.

26. Kornhauser, A. , Mental Health of the Industrial Worker,
     New York: Wiley, 1965.

27. Langner, T. S. and Michael, S. T. , Life Stress and
     Mental Health, Glencoe, Ill. : The Free Press,
     1963.

28. Manpower Report of the President, United States Depart-
     ment of Labor, General Printing Office, Superinten-
     dent of Documents, Washington, D. C. , April 1968,
     pp. 49, 3, 54.

29. Miller, D. C. and Form, W. H. , Industrial Sociology,
     New York: Harper, 1963.

30. National Science Foundation, Scientists, Engineers, and
     Technicians in the 1960s: Requirements and Supply,
     Washington, D. C. , pp. 63-64.

31. Parsons, Frank, Choosing a Vocation, Boston: Houghton
     Mifflin, 1909, p. 5.

32. Osipow, S. H. , Theories of Career Development, New
     York: Appleton-Century-Crofts, 1968.

33. Patterson, C. H. , "Counseling: Self-Clarification and
     the Helping Relationship, " in: Man in a World at
     Work, Boston: Houghton Mifflin, 1964.

34. Patterson, C. H. , The Counselor in the School, Selec-
     ted Readings, New York: McGraw-Hill, 1967, p.
     223.

35. Quey, R. L. , "Toward a Definition of Work, " Person-
     nel and Guidance Journal, November 1968, pp. 223-
     227.

36. Roe, Anne, "Early Determinants of Vocational Choice, "
     Journal of Counseling Psychology, 1957, vol. 4,
     pp. 212-217.

37. Roe, Anne, The Psychology of Occupations, New York:
     Wiley, 1956, p. 31.

38. Rogers, C. R. , "A Theory of Therapy, Personality
     and Interpersonal Relationships as Developed in the
     Client-Centered Framework, " in: Koch, S. , ed. ,

Psychology: A Study of Science, Study I; Conceptual and Systemic, Volume 3; Formulations of the Person and the Social Context, New York: McGraw-Hill, 1959.

39. Rogers, C. R. , "Psychometric Tests and Client-Centered Counseling, " Educational Psychological Measurements, 1946, vol. 6, pp. 139-144.

40. Schaffer, R. H. , "Job Satisfaction as Related to Need Satisfaction in Work, " Psychological Monographs, 1953, p. 67.

41. Schein, E. H. , "The First Job Dilemma, " Psychology Today, March 1968, vol. 1, pp. 26-37.

42. Super, D. E. , "Vocational Adjustment: Implementing of Self-Concept, " Occupations, 1951, pp. 30, 88, 92.

43. Super, D. E. , "A Theory of Vocational Development, " American Psychologist, 1953, vol. 8, pp. 185-190.

44. Super, D. E. , "Career Patterns as a Basis for Vocational Counseling, " Journal of Counseling Psychology, 1954, vol. 1, pp. 12-19.

45. Super, D. E. , The Psychology of Careers, New York: Harper, 1957, pp. 191, 197.

46. Super, D. E. , Career Development: Self-Concept Theory, New York: College Entrance Examination Board, 1963.

47. Thompson, A. S. , "Personality Dynamics and Vocational Counseling, " Personnel and Guidance Journal, 1960, vol. 38, pp. 350-357.

48. Thoroman, E. C. , The Vocational Counseling of Adults and Young Adults, Boston: Houghton Mifflin, 1968.

49. Tiedeman, D. V. , "Decision and Vocational Development, " Personnel and Guidance Journal, 1961, vol. 40, pp. 15-21.

50. Tiedeman, D. V. , Information Systems for Vocational Decisions, Second Annual Report, Harvard Graduate School of Education, Cambridge, Mass. , 1967-1968.

51. Tilgher, A., "Work Through the Ages," in: Nosow, S. and Form, W. H., eds., Men, Work and Society, New York: Basic Books, 1962.

52. Women's Bureau, U. S. Department of Labor, Wage and Labor Standards Administration, Washington, D. C. 69056, November 1968.

53. Wilensky, H. L., "Orderly Careers and Social Participation: The Impact of Work History on Social Integration in the Middle Mass," American Sociological Review, 1961, vol. 26, pp. 521-539.

54. Wilensky, H. L., "Varieties of Work Experience," in: Borow, Henry, ed., Man in a World at Work, Boston: Houghton Mifflin, 1964, pp. 125-154.

55. Williamson, E. G., "A Concept of Counseling," Occupations, 1950, vol. 29, pp. 182-189.

56. Williamson, E. G., "Value Orientation in Counseling," Personnel and Guidance Journal, 1958, vol. 37, pp. 520-528.

57. Williamson, E. G., Vocational Counseling: Some Historical, Philosophical and Theoretical Perspectives, New York: McGraw-Hill. 1965.

58. Wolfbeing, S., Employment and Unemployment in the United States, Chicago: Science Research Associates, 1964.

59. "Men Close Generation Gap," The New York Times, November 15, 1970.

Chapter V

SHORT-TERM COUNSELING

by Reuben R. McDaniel, Jr.

"Short-term counseling" for the purposes of this presentation, is defined as a one-to-one, or group contact of a short duration, between a counselor and a client population which assists the client to grow in order that he might deal with the presenting problem and with other problems in a more integrated fashion. Short-term counseling often occurs outside of the usual psychological setting and is sometimes a one-time encounter, although it can and may lead to subsequent, more traditional guidance contacts. The client should take from short-term counseling an increased capacity to deal with his environment in a constructive manner. Thus, it is viewed as one form of guidance and its goals are congruent with the general purposes of counseling. [4]

There are, however, some techniques which are of special interest to those who find themselves, through choice or necessity, engaged in this type of assistance for adults in a college setting. It is to these particular techniques that this presentation is offered.

Most counselor preparation today is directed toward helping him develop a methodology, a position vis-à-vis his client population, which is most useful when there is a continuous, sustained relationship between the client and counselor. A basic hypothesis of much of the literature in the field seems to be that there will be more than one meeting with the client and that these will be conducted in a setting in which the counselor will have access to records, anecdotal data, reference material, and so on. [3] There is, however, an increasing awareness that "ideal" conditions may not prevail for much of this counseling. As members of the profession recognize the need to make significant contact with a larger proportion of their potential client population, additional attention is being paid to ways in which the

78

counselor can relate to clients in settings other than the
"ideal" ones.   Counselors of adults have long recognized
that in their relationships with clients, often the best result
possible (although not the best possible result) is short-term
counseling.

It could be contended that the kind of "on-the-spot"
short-term relationships which characterize so many of the
contacts between the counselor of adults and his clients are
so totally unstructured and lack so many of the normal requi-
sites for a good counseling rapport that it is not proper to
call these encounters "counseling." If, however, this is defined in terms of client growth, and successful techniques
for promoting such growth in a short-term relationship can
be developed, then the potential for serving the adult population will be considerably enhanced.

Cottle and Downie in their book, Procedures and
Preparation for Counseling, state

> Successful counseling is based on a thorough knowl-
> edge of the factors affecting individual behavior and
> the ability to help a client understand and accept
> these factors so that they may play an appropriate
> part in future behavior. [1]

The authors further say, "...a counselor must be
able to relate to clients in a manner that inspires confidence
and trust that respects the integrity and capacities of the
client...."[2]   Certainly short-term counseling can be carried
out in such a way as to satisfy this criteria.

There are several significant factors which create a
need for short-term counseling relationships with adult students.   Each must be carefully considered by the counselor
as he develops a strategy for his work.

The first of these is that the adult student tends to
be reluctant to seek help from others in dealing with his
problems.   A sign of maturity in the folklore of American
life is that an adult can take care of himself.   Admitting to
another person that one needs help, particularly in the
areas of decision making, problem solving and personal
adjustment, is considered by many to be a sign of weakness
or immaturity.   The adult student often desires, above all,
to be considered a mature human being.   He is, therefore,
wary of seeking counseling assistance and this may cause

him to avoid the traditional counseling relationships.

A second factor which creates a need for short-term
counseling is the experience or lack thereof which the adult
may have had with counselors in his previous educational
programs.   The existence of well-trained and competent
professionals in the adult's previous educational setting must
not be taken for granted.   Many adults saw their high school
guidance personnel, for example, as persons who handled
discipline problems or devoted most of their energies to
pre-college counseling.   The adult, therefore, may view
the counselor as a person who would not be interested in
their concerns.   In situations where previous counseling relationships have been unsatisfactory or nonexistent, the adult
will have little reason to seek formal help.   He may, perhaps, find the unstructured setting of short-term counseling
a comfortable arrangement for conferring with others.   It
should allow him to test a situation before making what
might seem to him a threatening commitment to a counseling
relationship.

The life style of the adult student is the third factor
which may lead him to short-term counseling.   An adult
student is a busy person, living in a pressure situation.
Involved in earning a living and meeting family responsibilities as well as attending school, he seldom has the opportunity to use the campus for reflection, self-examination or
even informal social activities.   Normally, when the student
comes into the college environment, it is with a specific
goal in mind.   He may not even have considered the possibility that the campus might offer an opportunity for counseling assistance.   The fact that he has so little time and has
so many pressures on his life style, often means that short-
term counseling is the only kind of help the adult can receive.

The reluctant adult whose previous experience with
guidance is limited and whose life style leaves little time
for seeking help is, therefore, a prime candidate for short-
term counseling.   When an adult student feels uneasy in
his present job situation, he may feel that vocational expectations are outside of the school context except as a training
opportunity to increase his worth in the market place.   Previous experience may indicate to him that school counselors
can do little about job-related problems except to send him
to an employment office.   In addition, the student may feel
that he just does not have the time to spare to seek advice.

This particular person may find that an informal setting, such as a registration period, is a chance to say to a
counselor, "Do you think that I am too old to go to law
school?" This type of question is often an opportunity for
short-term counseling. The client has conquered his natural
reluctance to seek help by approaching the counselor in a
setting which makes the contact appear to be a casual one.
As unfair as it may seem to the professional, the client
may be using this informal setting to test the potential interest the counselor may or may not have in him and his
concerns. The contact is taking place in a situation which
requires little time commitment from the client and which
does not seriously interrupt his normal busy schedule. The
counselor may respond to the client's query about law school
in at least three ways, "yes," "no," or "why do you ask?"
While perhaps none of these is a perfect response, the
third is an open-ended one which may well lead to a discussion of a possible concern right on the spot. The counselor can avail himself of this chance to serve his client
through short-term counseling.

The counselor of adults should strive to increase the
number of settings which serve to encourage short-term
counseling relationships with his client population. Several
different kinds of situations may serve this purpose. For
example, he can involve himself in the planning of adult
student social events. By helping to create an atmosphere
in which students feel relaxed and at ease with the institution, with their fellow students and with the faculty and
staff, he will find that the students are more likely to approach him for short-term counseling. Orientation meetings, planned with adequate time for students and staff to
mix, give the counselor an opportunity to talk to groups of
students about common student concerns. Such meetings
serve to build rapport with the client population. Small
group meetings, called by the counselor to discuss specific
institutional concerns, provide another avenue for client
contact. Often large introductory sections of popular courses
are a good source of volunteers to work with the counselor
on a problem. When done on a one-shot basis and as an
honest attempt to receive student feedback on a serious issue, the adult student will generally be happy to co-operate.
Through these sessions, students learn to know the counsel-
or and see his real concern for their welfare. Participants
in the group, as well as those students with whom they discuss the meeting, are then more likely to approach him for
professional help. A counselor should constantly be search-

ing for other situations, perhaps peculiar to his own specific
environment, which lend themselves to this type of short-
term counseling.

The guidance office, if located near an area of high
student traffic, can also provide the setting for short-term
counseling.   While the majority of office contacts will be
made by appointment, some time should purposely be left
free for drop-in clients.   Careful thought should be given
to when adult students are more likely to seek him out to
avail themselves of his services.   For example, those students who take evening classes often arrive on campus 20
or 30 minutes before class.   The break between classes is
another time when students may be encouraged to drop in to
the counseling office.   If the counselor keeps specially selected times free from scheduled appointments and informs
the students of this, he is likely to find that the number of
drop-in meetings will increase.   Each of these certainly
provides an opportunity for establishing rapport and in a
surprising number of cases productive results occur.

Some students who come in to see a counselor by
appointment are essentially clients for short-term counseling.   A student who wants to know whether he should drop
a course is often prohibited by college regulations from taking the time required for sustained advisement.   He would
like to have some assistance in developing a solution to his
problem and he needs that help immediately.   The counselor
must avoid the sharp accusation, "Why didn't you come in
sooner?", and instead work with the problem within the
time constraints imposed.   If this is to be done without im-
posing the counselor's will on the client or substituting
counselor-judgment, then careful attention must be paid to
the techniques of this kind of counseling.

Often it is difficult to recognize some of the counseling opportunities that are presented.   While it is generally
a sound technique to deal with the presenting problem, i-
dentifying that problem is not always easy.   This is particularly true when clients come to the counselor's office with
what may seem an overly straightforward concern.   A student may come in and say that he is being transferred out-
of-town by his employer and will have to drop out of school.
At other times, the conference can be a true search for assistance.   The student may be anxious about his educational
future in light of the impending transfer.   There may be concerns about the relocation of his family or the unfamiliar

responsibilities the new position will entail. The counselor
of adults must learn to catch these nuances if they are present without unnecessary intrusion into the lives of his clients.

Counselors must be "where the students are" and
they must be available for assisting them. When the counselor is busy at registration, setting up schedules for students who need immediate program-planning help, he may
then possibly lose many opportunities for short-term counseling. If, however, it can be arranged to have faculty advisors or upper-class students helping with course-planning,
then the counselor will be free to circulate among the students, talk informally with them and, in general, remain
alert for situations demanding his specialized talents. Registration periods can be extremely stressful times for students.
New students who are unsure of themselves often see the
maze of forms, directions, lines, cards, etc., as formidable
barriers to their educational opportunities. Other students
may be concerned about getting into a specific course that
they need for their program or a particular section with a
well-known professor. These situations usually do not demand a long, therapeutic counseling relationship. They are,
however, situations in which supportive short-term counseling is appropriate. If the counselor of adults can make himself available at these times, he can provide a significant
service to his client population.

He should not wait for an "event" in order to make
himself available to any and all students. Being seen in
the school corridors three or four times a term during coffee breaks or changes of class can lead to a more open relationship between student and counselor. Periodic visits
to the snack shop, the library or any other place where
adult students congregate to relax, complain and generally
"let off steam" help to create an atmosphere which may
lead to quests for guidance. Those who make themselves
available on a regularly planned basis where students are
will find that they are providing opportunities for much pre-
ventive work. They will increase the likelihood that their
potential contribution will be understood by the client population. This is, indeed, an important part of the responsibilities of the counselor of adults.

There is a need for the creation of opportunities in
which short-term counseling can be facilitated. The counsel-
or must make a careful review of the potential within his
particular environment. He must not be so hurried that an

important opening is overlooked, or that possible counseling
associations with the client population are blocked. In addition, the counselor must be prepared to deal with unstructured and unplanned relationships. What then are some of
the critical techniques of short-term counseling? While
many of them have been implied in the preceding discussion,
specific attention should be given to a few of the more significant.

The counselor of adults must become increasingly
sensitive to both his clients and to his own potential as a
change agent outside of his office. Although most counselors
certainly prepare carefully for planned sessions with students,
many seem to lose the sensitive edge when they leave their
offices.

Knowledge of the client population, the second factor,
is especially critical in the informal setting which often
characterizes short-term counseling. Student files and other
specific data are usually not available. It is important,
therefore, that the counselor build, in his mind, a summary
profile of his client population for use in the unstructured
situation. The students should never be stereotyped on the
basis of average population characteristics, but the ability
of the counselor to recognize how they might fit into or
deviate from the general pattern is especially helpful.

The third critical factor is rapport, particularly because short-term counseling is often conducted in most unsatisfactory physical surroundings. It is difficult to establish
a sympathetic relationship when standing at registration, and
while informality may be easy in the snack shop, counseling
rapport is not. Perhaps the primary factor which can enhance a harmonious short-term counseling relationship is a
human characteristic which best might be described as gen-
tleness. If the counselor is gentle as opposed to abrupt,
harsh, or perhaps in too much of a hurry, then rapport can
be established more quickly.

The fourth technique, and one which is particularly
useful, is observation. It is necessary that special attention be paid to the physical appearance of the client, especially with respect to possible agitation. For example, does
the client ask what seems to be a normal kind of question
in a highly confidential tone of voice? Does it seem that he
is particularly apologetic as he expresses a problem or concern? The counselor must observe his client in an extremely

keen manner if clues to counseling are to be used.

It is important in short-term counseling that the client believes that he is being understood and, therefore, feedback is the fifth critical factor. It is tempting to rush past meaningful feedback and move on to some kind of problem solution when there is an informal setting and time is limited. It is, however, essential, under conditions where the client himself may be testing the relationship in what is to him a nonthreatening atmosphere, that the counselor provide the understanding and clarification of feeling which characterize good feedback.

Planning, with the client, is as important in short-term counseling as it is in more traditional counseling styles and is the sixth critical technique. If the client leaves the contact feeling that he has at least a tentative plan for further action, then he will have achieved an increased sense of order and direction. If, however, he sees no plan for future activity, then he may feel that the situation has been chaotic and unhelpful.

The closing of a short-term counseling interview is extremely significant and, therefore, is the seventh crucial factor. While the situation may be informal and accelerated, it is necessary that the relationship be terminated in an open-ended fashion. One of the most obvious truths about short-term counseling proves that it is best when it leaves the client with the feeling that further meetings with the counselor might be profitable. Careful attention to closing techniques will help achieve this goal.

There are, then, these seven criteria to be considered by the short-term counselor of adults:

1. Sensitivity to the situation
2. Knowledge of the client population
3. Ability to establish rapport quickly
4. Observation of the client
5. Feedback to the client
6. Planning with the client
7. Open-ended closing of the interview

The generalized goals of short-term counseling are comparatively easy to identify. This type of encounter might certainly be the entree to a more formal and structured long-term counseling relationship. Clients who may not come to the office, or whose problems are such that they would not normally be referred, should find that the informal contact, through an orientation program or a registration period, is the opening of the door to a meaningful long-term counseling relationship.

Referral is another possible goal. While a 5-, 10- or 15-minute contact may seem much too short for the counselor to determine that a referral is in order, there are many instances where such an action is clearly in order. If, for example, the counseling contact involves what is a vocational concern, then the client might well be referred immediately to the vocational guidance office. If the referral can be made right at the point of the initial interview, even if that contact is an informal one, then it is more likely to be followed through by the client. When the referral is delayed until a more structured counseling situation can be arranged, the client may well feel that his needs are immediate and, as a person in a pressure situation with little time, he will not appreciate this kind of dalliance.

Of course, the counseling may be terminated right after short-term counseling. Two things should be apparent to the counselor if he decides that closing is the most desirable sequent. The first of these is counselee growth. It is indeed possible, if the counselor is sensitive to the short-term relationship, to see the client's growth in a very brief period of time. Many adult clients experience meaningful insights into themselves and their relationship with their environment as a result of brief encounters with well-trained counselors. This is particularly true when the client needed either a certain degree of reassurance or some well-thought-out advice. The second thing which must be present if closing is in order is a feeling on the part of the client that he is willing and prepared to terminate. In short, the counselor and the client should experience a degree of satisfaction concerning the relationship which indicates it should be terminated.

Training in the methodology of short-term counseling is necessary if this technique is to be a valuable tool to the counselor of adults. Practicum experiences should be developed which permit supervisors to assist beginning counselors. Such situations would be difficult to structure, but serious consideration should be given to some possibilities. Role-playing short-term counseling relationships are helpful. Practicum field experiences, observed by the supervisor, would give the beginning counselor an opportunity to test his techniques. The use of video tapes to observe the activities of counselors in situations which might lend an insight to short-term counseling is a possibility. In-service training programs for the counselors of adults should certainly include some exposure to the feasible uses and benefits of these techniques.

Clearly related to training is the development of case histories for short-term counseling activities. It is difficult, especially when one is away from the convenience of the office, to develop a meaningful case history. The conscientious counselor, however, will make on-the-spot notations about one-to-one or group encounters that he experiences in nonstructured situations. When these notations are reviewed, often follow-up activity is indicated. These notations can also serve as the core of case conferences which cover the experiences of a staff at such a time as student orientation or registration.

In conclusion, it would be well to look at some of the significant questions which must be asked about short-term counseling. The first of these involves the role of the faculty. How many of the one-to-one and group contacts which they have with adult students, particularly outside of the classroom, could be enhanced by additional training in short-term counseling techniques? As a primary part of this question, it would be well to explore the faculty's knowledge and use of the referral process.

A second question is the training and use of paraprofessionals in short-term counseling. Particularly, can they help as facilitators of the entire counseling program for adult students?

The effectiveness of short-term counseling needs to be carefully researched. Is this seemingly a stop-gap measure which is being used only because of a lack of adequate staff or has it been an effective means of counseling communication with clients and a genuine help in achieving client growth?

The immediate future of short-term counseling seems to be clear. It does not appear that within the near future there will be enough counselors of adults nor enough acceptance on the part of the potential client population to confine counseling to the techniques and advantages of the long-term relationship. As more and more adult students enter educational institutions and as the staffing of counseling centers becomes more and more difficult, it becomes increasingly apparent that the counselor of adults must search for ways to make his role more effective. Short-term counseling offers such an eventuality.

References

1. Cottle, W. C., and Downie, N. M., Procedures and Preparation for Counseling, Englewood Cliffs, N. J.: Prentice-Hall, 1960, p. 7 (330 pp).

2. Ibid.

3. See: Patterson, C. H., Theories of Counseling and Psychotherapy, New York: Harper and Row, 1966 (518 pp).

4. Rogers, C. R., Counseling and Psychotherapy, Boston: Houghton Mifflin, 1942, p. 28 (450 pp).

Chapter VI

COUNSELING THE GRADUATE STUDENT

by Kenneth H. Sproull

The purpose of this chapter is to identify and discuss some of the pressures and conflicts leading to counseling problems of graduate students. In addition, the chapter is concerned with establishing the need for specialized counseling services at the graduate level.

If the establishment of such services seems questionable, one has only to review the literature to find that little has been written about counseling for the graduate student. Although there is an abundance of literature ranging from elementary counseling to counselor education programs, it would appear that graduate students ignore their peers when conducting research and, worse yet, professors ignore their own products which contributes to many of the frustrations of graduate students.

Kaback notes that "too little time has been spent in developing a philosophy of counseling for the adult [or graduate] student."[3] Farmer, in discussing counseling services in institutions of higher education, indicates that the "counseling programs in many of them have been geared for the adolescent or undergraduate student."[1]

Thompson observes that not only is the adult or graduate student all but neglected completely but he also differs in many respects from the adolescent or undergraduate.[7] There are obvious differences in age, self-concept, background, experiences and goal orientation. Although graduate students' counseling needs may be similar to those of students at other levels of education, they are greatly intensified. Despite these many differences, heightened pressures, and unique problems, and possibly because of the graduate student's maturity and academic success, we have provided only minimum services to meet their needs.

No Counselor for the Graduate Student

Graduate students feel that there is no counselor or faculty member that they can turn to with their personal problems while attending graduate school. This feeling may be partially a result of the students' own fears and perceptions and/or partially the fault of the institution for not providing a specific counselor for the graduate student. Graduate students, more than undergraduate students, are reluctant to seek help in solving their personal problems. They fear that any exposure of their "weakness" may filter back to their department or major professor and affect their academic progress. This possibility can be particularly threatening for students in specific fields such as psychology and education where the counselor or advisor also teaches courses in which the graduate student may enroll. Therefore, although "a counselor" may be available to the graduate student on campus, the likelihood of the student using the service is minimal unless the service is designed specifically for him.

Graduate Education

It is indeed unfortunate that the very programs, processes and procedures of graduate education, including constant evaluation, mitigate the establishment of trust and confidence needed to encourage the graduate student to discuss his personal problems with existing counselors or faculty advisors. The high drop-out and suicide rate of graduate students attests to the possibility that all is not well in graduate education.

Rogers, in discussing graduate education in his book Freedom to Learn, writes, "When we examine what we do rather than what we profess in this area [graduate education in psychology] the picture which emerges is, in my estimation, a sorry one."[6] One suspects that the field of psychology is not atypical of graduate education in general.

Graduate education, including the curriculum, teaching methods, examinations, pressure for grades, and impersonal faculty, is in need of reform. In its present form on many campuses, graduate students experience only frustration and a high level of anxiety. There appears to be a real need to provide the mature, adult graduate student with a different educational experience including specialized student personnel services to enhance his personal growth as well as his academic progress.

However, beyond the pressures of the academic program are other problems which graduate students indicate
affect the successful completion of their graduate degrees.

Financial Pressure

One of the first problems that confronts the graduate
student is how he will finance his graduate education. They
are often unaware of the financial aspects of graduate school
and of the available financial resources. Their undergraduate
education was financed by or through parental support, sav-
ings, scholarships, loans, and part-time work. With the
baccalaureate degree earned, the financial resources available
to the student are often exhausted. In addition, the graduate
student is at an age where he wants to be "his own man, "
free from parental influence and financial assistance. He
may be already married or be thinking of marriage. If married, children may add not only to the cost of his education
but a whole range of frustrations including baby sitting, study
conditions and the normal problems of adjustment as a newly-
wed.

Oppelts' study concerning married students indicated
that over 50 per cent of the married men involved in his
survey rated finances as their major source of problems.
His study also revealed that married students also worked
more hours and had greater debts than unmarried students. [5]

However, even the single graduate student must make
financial sacrifices to complete his graduate program. Making ends meet for both the married and single student while
foregoing immediate employment to satisfy personal needs
and desires can be frustrating for many and may cause the
end or delay of graduate school participation.

Living Conditions

Many students enroll for graduate school at institutions other than the college from which they received their
baccalaureate degree. These "new" students arrive on campus with little or no orientation concerning the institution or
services such as those offered to the entering freshman. The
graduate student arrives on campus alone and must often
shift for himself. If undergraduate residence halls are a-
vailable, the graduate student rejects this style of living
and seeks off-campus housing.

For various reasons, the graduate student may live off-campus, alone and in substandard housing. For financial reasons, he may later share a room or apartment with one or more students enrolled in different fields and with different needs and interests. Thus, the graduate student may live in the midst of thousands and still live "alone" forming few close relationships with others. The lack of financial resources, living off-campus, and the demands of graduate school often isolate the graduate student either by choice or circumstance. This condition contributes to his need to communicate with others concerning his present problems and future concerns.

Expectations

Many students are poorly informed concerning the life of the graduate student. They have conquered the jungle of undergraduate school and enter graduate work with the expectation that things will be different. They anticipate a new type of learning experience and a closer relationship with the graduate faculty in their major field.

For many graduate students, eager expectations turn into complete disappointment when they encounter the same system of lectures, tests, papers and grades. He is exposed to some of the poorest teaching per se experienced at any level of our educational system. In addition, he must adhere to a bureaucratic system of procedures and deadlines to ultimately receive the good graces and sanction of the university in proclaiming he is one of their graduates and, more important, a contributing alumnus. It is little wonder that so many excellent students drop out of graduate school because their expectations were not met.

The Bureaucracy

It has been said that we can do almost anything to a freshman. We can require batteries of tests, enforce rules and regulations, let him endure long waiting lines and suffer whatever else the faculty and administration feels is necessary for enrollment.

The graduate student, older and more mature, may find the procedures, designed for the mass of undergraduate students, inappropriate to his needs. How many times does he have to inform the registrar of his race, religion, sex, and citizenship? One of the by-products of our educational system is the creativity demonstrated by many graduate students in "beating the system." Instead of teaching the graduate student to learn the system as an educational experience, we might better design procedures to meet his needs.

Foreign Students

The enrollment of foreign students in American colleges and universities has approximately doubled in the last decade. Their numbers will increase in the years ahead and many of these will be graduate students. McCann notes that orientation to the university and the larger culture, language proficiency, and financial support all contribute to adjustment problems experienced by the foreign student. Like their American counterpart, the foreign student often rejects residence hall living which includes roommates, inappropriate menus, and intolerable study conditions. [4]

Beyond these more obvious problems confronted by the foreign student are those human needs described by Gilsdorf as the need for companionship, recognition and approval. [2] The foreign student arrives on our campuses leaving behind family, friends, language, tradition, culture, and sometimes his wife and children. He hopes, consciously or unconsciously, to find a friendly group of people. Soon he realizes that in the student community there is little place for him. His lack of English language proficiency makes it difficult to initiate a conversation due to the fear of making language mistakes.

All of this adds up to what Gilsdorf calls the foreign student's "loneliness." [2] Although American students and faculty members could alleviate this feeling of seclusion, special counseling services and programs are needed to assist the foreign student with his multiple problems.

Placement

As graduation day approaches for our students, we, as educators, feel that our products are capable of accepting positions of responsibility in the world of work. However, the "real world" can be extremely frightening for the graduate student. He has feelings of inadequacy and is concerned about his lack of experience. After years of formal preparation, he knows little about "how to get a job."

Many institutions of higher education offer little or no

assistance to the graduate student seeking employment. They
abandon the student just at the most crucial period of his
life. It is then that he needs counsel, advice, support and
assistance if he is to make appropriate career decisions.

The Known and Unknown

Other areas of stress and frustration that confront
the graduate student have been discussed in preceding chapters concerning the "adult" student. The graduate student
shares with the adult student the same frustrations by functioning within an educational system designed for the adolescent or undergraduate student.

One can only speculate at this point in time what impact current issues such as the military draft, the war,
Black Power and campus unrest may have upon graduate education and the graduate student. Although the graduate student may be less likely than an undergraduate to participate
in student protest directed toward the "establishment" and
the system, he may hope to gain much from legitimate and
needed change in higher education.

A New Emphasis

Student personnel services such as orientation, registration, housing, financial aids and activities are essentially
geared to serving the undergraduate student. Graduate enrollments are reaching the level where it is financially
feasible and, more important, humane, to provide specialized
services for graduate students. In particular, the existing
literature and informal student surveys would suggest that a
planned program of counseling services is needed to assist
the graduate student to successfully complete his academic
graduate program.

The major areas of concern for graduate students,
beyond those of the existing academic program, would suggest specialized services to meet their needs. As a minimum, colleges and universities offering graduate programs
could:

    1.   Provide one or more counselors to work specifi-
        cally with graduate students.

    2.   Provide within the counselor education program
        appropriate background and training for those

wishing to work in the area of graduate and foreign student counseling.

3. Provide appropriate housing or housing services to meet the needs of the graduate student.

4. Provide procedures within existing offices and/ or separate services to minimize red tape to accommodate the adult graduate student.

5. Provide job placement services for the graduate student.

Conclusion

History, particularly in recent years, has demonstrated that needed reform in higher education occurs most frequently when students protest loud enough, long enough, and unfortunately, sometimes, violently enough. Before confrontation, protest, and violence, it behooves those of us involved in student personnel work to develop programs and services designed to meet the specific needs of the adult graduate student.

In general, students are winning the battle for freedom of speech, press, civil rights, and liberation from the archaic rules and regulations still in effect in many institutions of higher education. Without question, the student of the future will turn his attention to the inadequacies and weaknesses of the educational process itself including the relevance of the curriculum, instructional methods, and student personnel services.

More specifically, as graduate enrollments increase, student personnel services, such as orientation, housing, financial aid, and placement, need to be fitted to the needs of the mature adult graduate student within or separate from existing programs presently designed to meet the needs of the undergraduate student.

References

1. Farmer, Martha L., "Counseling Adult Students," ACPA: Proceedings of a Pre-Convention Workshop, Counseling the Adult Student, a Report of Commission XIII, March 1967, pp. 21-27.

2. Gilsdorf, Louis, "Americans Don't Realize the Foreign Student's Loneliness," The Western Catalyst, Western Illinois University, May 19, 1970, p. 1.

3. Kaback, Goldie Ruth, "Counseling: The Counselor Vis-à-vis the Counselee," ACPA: Proceedings of a Pre-Convention Workshop, College Personnel Services for the Adult, a Report of Commission XIII, April 1968, pp. 27-32.

4. McCann, Carolyn J., "Major Issues in Advising Foreign Students: A Review," Journal of the National Association of Women Deans and Counselors, Vol. 27, No. 4, 1964, pp. 172-178.

5. Oppelts, Norman T., "Characteristics and Activities of Married College Students," The Journal of College Student Personnel, Vol. 6, No. 4, June 1965, pp. 86-89.

6. Rogers, Carl R., Freedom to Learn, Columbus, Ohio: Charles E. Merrill Pub. Co., 1969, p. 170.

7. Thompson, Clarence H., "The Nature of the Adult Student," ACPA: Proceedings of a Pre-Convention Workshop, Counseling the Adult Student, a Report of Commission XIII, March 1967, pp. 1-11.

Chapter VII

FINANCIAL AID COUNSELING

by Martha L. Farmer

Financial aid counseling is generally held to be an
important part of the student personnel services of institutions of higher learning. There are those who subscribe to
this philosophy only for the full-time adolescent student as
they feel the adult student does not need financial counseling. Their rationale is that the adult is self-supporting and
is capable of managing his own financial affairs. This
point-of-view is often strengthened when the counselor is
younger than the adult student who seeks his assistance, and
may have little knowledge of the adult's life style and needs.

The adults who enter higher education are often employed at a marginal salary. Many of their problems have
roots in deep and frustrating difficulties in making ends
meet. They may have families to support or in the case of
younger adults they must contribute to the family's support.
The mere fact that they have entered college is indicative
of their desire to move out of dead-end employment in
which they find themselves.

The cost of their education often puts a serious drain
on the family budget. Loss of a job, unexpected medical
expenses, leaving home in the case of the younger adults,
and other upheavals often produce a crisis situation in which
they may consider dropping out of school. If they have a
financial aid counselor to whom they can turn for advice and
assistance, this course of action can often be averted.

It is essential that the financial aid counselor of
adults have access to loan and/or grant funds specifically
set up for this purpose. In this way, he is in a position
to evaluate the student's real need in terms of being able
to draw up a realistic budget and to provide financial assistance which will aid the student in resolving the crisis.

An example of this is the case of a woman in her early twenties who had left home to move into a small place of her own. Her family lived in a slum area of the city with its concomitant physical disintegration and harassment. She borrowed money from an evening short-term loan fund to pay part of her tuition. When she stopped repaying her loan, the financial aid counselor sent for her. He learned that in addition to buying meager furniture on time, she had also been enticed into purchasing (on so-called excellent terms) a $175. 00 stereo hi-fi set. When she lost her job, her lack of experience in budgeting had gotten her into a position in which she could see no way out of her dilemma. The counselor extended the time of repayment of her loan, found employment for her on the campus and helped her to draw up a realistic budget. She was able to remain in college and finally became a full-time student.

It is essential that the financial aid counselor be a-vailable at the time the adult is in attendance at the college, at a scheduled time during the evening hours. Unfortunately, too many counselors are available only from 9 to 4 during the day session of the college. Few adults can afford to take time off from their work to seek financial advice which may cost them a half-day's pay. In cases of mothers with dependent children who are on welfare, it means that they must bring their children with them, as money for baby sitters is seldom provided by the agency. These women often attend college during the evening when they can arrange to have friends stay with the children.

The inner-city adult frequently is in particular need of financial aid counseling. The life style of many of these students is, at times, on a bare subsistence level. Their places of residence are often in dilapidated old-law tenements. More than one family may occupy a deteriorating apartment. They are accustomed to living on the brink of economic disaster. Many of their purchases are made on time or through loans from finance companies which charge them outrageous rates of interest, thus keeping them at a continuing poverty level. Adults who enter college from this group often have unrealistic ideas of the cost of courses they wish to take. For this reason, they may borrow more money from college loan funds, where they are available, than they realistically can repay within the time specified. Even though many states are involved in federally guaranteed loan programs, individuals from minority groups are often refused loans from local banks because they are considered poor risks.

Many times, the adult's classification as other than a full-time student makes him ineligible for state incentive grants, scholarships or loans. As a result, the only limited funds they can call on are those of the institution they are attending.

Many financial aid counselors feel that federal and state funds are better spent on full-time adolescent students who have a reasonable chance of completing their academic careers within a specified length of time. It is, therefore, essential that the financial counseling of adults be an integral part of the financial aid structure of the institution. If the "one university" concept (combining day and evening sessions), which is gaining acceptance at institutions of higher learning, is to be valid, particular attention must be paid to the adult student, who will generally attend during the evening hours. Financial aid for the adult cannot be a simple process of filling out a form and obtaining a loan. It is only through a face-to-face relationship with the counselor that a real loan program can be worked out which takes into consideration the total financial status of the adult student.

Procedure for Evaluation of Need

Many financial aid counselors develop their own procedures for evaluating the financial needs of the adult student. Some use the "Student's Confidential Statement" of the College Scholarship Service adapting it to the counselor's own needs so that it will reflect a true picture of the financial plight of the adult student. If the students are married, employed, have children, drive cars, or own houses or pay rent, their parent's income, usually pertinent in adolescent full-time student loans, has no relevance. Whatever type of evaluation form is used, it should provide the financial aid counselor with appropriate information so that he can ascertain the basic adult needs.

At colleges where such forms must be filled out several weeks prior to registration, it is possible to ask for complete information which can be acted upon before the student registers. When a student requires a loan at the time of registration, a less complicated form would be more practical. The latter are usually institutional short-term loans which must be repaid within the semester. In this case, there is usually no money changing hands, but the student is given a credit chit which will be accepted by

the bursar.   These chits are redeemed by the financial aid
counselor or they are used to draw against funds previously
deposited by him with the bursar.

When the adult student wishes a longer-term state or
federal loan for which he is eligible, he must fill out the
appropriate form, generally a semester prior to the receipt
of the loan.   There is usually a limitation on monies available dependent upon the degree of participation by the institution in the particular program, and the amount ear-marked
for the adult student.   Some colleges require that a student
must complete a minimum number of credits before he is
eligible to receive a loan or grant.

Loan and Grant Funds for the Adult Student

It is not an easy task to obtain loan and grant funds
for adult students.   Traditionally, colleges have used their
funds almost exclusively for the full-time younger students.
Alumni and foundation grants have been made available to
this latter group.   It is only when funds are specifically
designated for the adult student that this ever-increasing
older student body is able to obtain financial assistance.
The full-time younger student can obtain a loan and grant
package made up from state, federal and institutional funds.
It is practically impossible for the adult because of his part-
time student status to be eligible for such extensive assistance.

Those institutions which have set up special loan and
grant funds for adults have found that it is possible to ad-
minister them more effectively through financial aid counseling.   The combination of a loan together with an outright
grant enables the adult realistically to plan his educational
expenses in relation to his overall economic needs.   The
adult often needs financial aid counseling to assist him
through the new experience of attending college while working to support himself or his family.

Special Categories of Adult Students

One of the handicaps experienced by the financial aid
counselor of adults is the general lack of information about
the available loans.   It is, therefore, essential that the
counselor explore all possibilities for financial aid if he is
to truly be effective in providing this service for an ever-
expanding adult student body.

Certain institutions have been able to obtain special funds from foundations to make loans and grants to special categories of students such as women who are entering or returning to higher education. Various women's organizations have been particularly effective in gaining support for this category of adults. State offices of continuing education in cooperation with participating colleges, both two-year and four-year, have effectively channeled those women who sought its assistance from their local guidance centers into colleges. The women's bureaus of many states have also worked to make possible the entry of women financially into higher education.

Graduate Students

Graduate students of late have been hard pressed to find financial assistance. The brilliant are competed for by various institutions each trying to offer greater financial aid than its rivals. The graduate students without outstanding credentials are therefore hard-pressed to find fellowships, scholarships and loans to meet the ever-increasing cost of tuition.

Many graduate schools are now using an evaluation sheet of the student's needs as a means of determining eligibility. The inflationary spiral in the cost of higher education does not make this an easy task. Graduate students must often prolong their study because of the necessity to work part-time in order to make ends meet. This is particularly true of the married student who, although his wife may work, must also contribute to the support of their children. [3]

The shrinking of federal funds which formerly provided scholarships and grants has made competition even greater for those still available. The need for faculty in various academic disciplines has led subsequently to the disillusionment of many graduate students trained in these areas.

The financial aid counselors of graduate students are faced with an ever-increasing problem of finding financial support for these candidates. They must vigorously seek funds to assist them. A booklet of available grants, scholarships, fellowships and loans from all sources should be given to the prospective or already enrolled graduate student. An opportunity should be provided for in-depth inter-

views with the concerned candidates. With the increased difficulties faced by many of these individuals, financial aid
counseling should become a continuing process. A graduate
student once accepted by a university should be given a maximum chance of completing his degree.

Foreign Students

The foreign adult students often have greater problems
than average native-born or naturalized adults in our institutions of higher learning. The financial support previously
made available to them by sponsoring agencies has diminished
or disappeared in recent years.

Many schools are requiring a detailed financial-need
evaluation before accepting the foreign student. A common
rule-of-thumb ascertains that the student is proved to be
completely self-supporting during his first year at the college, before he can be considered for admission.[4] The
changing political structure of foreign nations has made such
an evaluation doubly important. Many foreign students, both
graduate and undergraduate, have found themselves without
funds when their government support has been withdrawn due
to a change of regime. In addition, some of these students
are unable to return home for political reasons and, as a
consequence, become stateless people.

The financial aid counselor must often spend a great
deal of time with them because of the depth of their problems.[5] Their different life styles and language patterns
must be given due consideration. The psychological impact
of the American culture often has a deleterious effect on
their ability to achieve academic success in our colleges and
universities. The counselor and foreign-student advisor must
work together closely to maximize the foreign students'
chances of survival in our institutions.

Veterans

The Veterans Readjustment Benefit Act of 1966, together with subsequent amendments, has made available full-
three-quarter and half-time educational assistance to qualifying veterans at institutions of higher learning. Funds are
also provided for tutorial assistance to veterans in academic
difficulties. It should be remembered that many of these
adults do not have cash available to pay for tuition, books
and living expenses when they initially enter college. The

financial aid counselor can render real help to veterans by making short or long-term loans so that the student can meet his obligations prior to receiving his V. A. check. Also, he can make sure that the student has filled out the required forms in the proper manner. The Veterans Administration sometimes claims that payments to recipients are delayed because of errors in filling out these documents.

With some exceptions, widows of veterans who died as a result of military service, as well as wives of totally or permanently disabled veterans are eligible for educational assistance. War-orphan training programs are also included in this law. When there is a question concerning entitlement, they should be referred to the local office of the Veterans Administration for clarification.

Members of the Armed Forces on active duty, who have served at least two years, may receive fee and tuition reimbursement.

Many veterans also take out National Defense Education Act student loans to supplement their GI benefits. The Elementary and Secondary School Act of 1970 (Public Law 91-230) provides that veterans who receive such loans may cancel 12. 5 per cent of their indebtedness for each year of military service up to a maximum of four years, but not to exceed one-half of their total indebtedness. [6]

Law Enforcement Officers

The Law Enforcement Education Program (LEEP) grants are available at participating institutions. These grants are made to officers and those who wish to join publicly-funded law enforcement agencies. These students enroll in police science, correction programs and related courses. They must also agree to remain with the sponsoring agency at least two years.

Social Security Benefits

Title II of the Social Security Act (revised) makes possible financial assistance for education ranging from $64. 00 to $140. 00 per month. [7] The financial aid counselor should be aware that some adult students may qualify since the ages covered are from 18 to 22 years. This, combined with other loans and grants, often makes it possible for the qualifying student to attend college on a full-time basis.

Community Oriented Programs

The community oriented programs are providing the
entree into higher education for many disadvantaged adults.
These potential students, for the most part, attend the evening division of participating colleges. The financial aid
counselor should know how these proposals are worded and
funded so that he can make this information available to currently enrolled or prospective students. It should be remembered that many programs require annual funding by the appropriate governmental legislative bodies. These programs
include Model Cities, New Careers, Community Action Agency, Work Incentive (WIN), Opportunities Industrialization
Centers (CIC) and many others. [10]

The various loans and grants provided for by the
Higher Education Act (revised in 1965) will not be dealt with
in this chapter since they are well documented in a number
of other publications. The financial aid officer should, however, keep in mind that adult students are eligible for this
type of assistance if they meet the qualifications set down by
Congress.

The Federally Insured Low Interest Loan Programs
and state corporations set up for this purpose are also well
documented in many publications and brochures. In those
states in which corporations have been established, such as
the Higher Education Assistance Corporation of New York
State, disadvantaged adults appear to be able to obtain loans
for education more easily than those states in which such
corporations have not been established.

It should be noted that both Presidents Johnson and
Nixon have attempted to phase out National Defense student
loans and transfer the student loans to the guaranteed loan
program. Congress, however, has rejected these presi-
dential recommendations and has continued to fund the NDSL
loan program.

The Educational Opportunity Bank "idea," which is
again being proposed by the Assembly on University Goals
and Governances as "Educaid," is worthy of study. The
principle of Educaid is to allow students capable of achieving academic success in college, regardless of economic
status, to borrow money under a deferred-payment plan.
These payments would be guaranteed by the Federal Government in much the same way that FHA mortgages are handled.

The students would repay these loans through their income
taxes over a 30-year period at a fixed percentage of their
annual incomes.   Those with higher incomes would pay back
more than those with low or nonexistent incomes (as in the
case of married women). [1]

This type of proposal in various forms has been
turned down several times by Congress.   Of late, Yale
University has indicated that it would experiment with a
"tuition-postponement option".   The Ford Foundation has
also expressed interest in this kind of student loan plan. [9]

This proposal should be of interest to adult students
if loans are made available to those attending on a part-
time basis.   As pointed out previously, many adults cannot
afford to attend college on a full-time basis because of
family support and concomitant responsibilities.

Loans, Grants, Scholarships and Tuition-Aid Plans

Individual institutions have their own unique programs
which are quite apart from those established by the state and
federal governments.   Not all loans and grants herein described are available at all colleges.   It is, therefore, helpful to mention some of these sources of financial aid which
may be offered exclusively to the adult student.   The list
is by no means all-inclusive, as individual schools may
have funds which are peculiar to them and/or of local
derivation.

This financial aid generally falls into several categories:

1.   Local business or professional association loan funds.
     These may be short-term loans repayable within the
     semester or they may be extended interest-free loans
     repayable upon graduation or separation from the
     college.

2.   Scholarship funds, established in much the same way
     as loan funds.   These scholarships are generally
     limited in number.   The recipient must have evi-
     denced ability and interest in specific areas, for
     example, real estate, transportation and traffic,
     urban affairs, engineering, or architecture.   Some
     local chapters of Alpha Sigma Lambda, the national
     evening student honor society, give scholarships.

The United States Association of Evening Students
also makes annual awards to its members.

3. Alumni association loan and grant funds, where
    specifically set up for adult students, are meeting
    a real need.   In the past, a great proportion of
    alumni funds went into financial aid for full-time
    students during the day.   The Alumni Association
    of The City College, CUNY, and the City College
    Fund of that institution are unique in their establish-
    ment of grant and loan funds for evening students.
    The Alumni Association's Heyman Fund, used en-
    tirely for grants, is replenished each semester. It
    has enabled many students from the inner city, who
    would otherwise have had to drop out of college be-
    cause of lack of funds, to continue their education.
    Through the combined use of these two funds, it is
    possible to juxtapose loans and grants in such a way
    that the recipient can repay the loan during the cur-
    rent semester.

4. A number of colleges have various plans under which
    people 65 years or older may attend college at a re-
    duced tuition.   These individuals are required gener-
    ally to pay only half the course cost charge.

5. There are some institutions which are accepting
    "Master Charge" and "BankAmericard" credit cards
    to pay tuition fees.   This, in essence, provides the
    student with his own deferred payment plan.   It,
    also, eliminates the school's cost of processing and
    collecting loans.   It should be pointed out, however,
    that this system works well when the students have
    such credit cards.   Many students from poverty areas
    are unable to obtain this type of credit.

6. Cooperative education plans, if expanded to include
    adult students, could meet many of their financial
    needs.   This would be particularly important if
    work related to academic objectives could be given
    college credit, thus lessening the time the adult
    would have to spend to complete his degree.   P. C.
    Li, in a study of the employment of evening part-
    time students, found that their responses to his
    questionnaire corroborated this point of view.   He
    found that 75 per cent of those employed in fields
    related to their college majors intended to remain

with their employers after graduation; 20 per cent
did not and the remaining 5 per cent were undecided.
He suggests that work-study programs for adults be
expanded to provide meaningful cooperative educational
experiences. 2, 9

7. Tuition Aid plans have become an integral part of
    fringe benefits offered by many industries.   These
    tuition-remission plans vary according to the philoso-
    phy of the particular company.   The financial aid
    counselor should keep a portfolio of the tuition aid
    possibilities in his locale.   He should solicit indus-
    tries' cooperation in establishing a working relation-
    ship between the college and the particular compan-
    ies.   The counselor should visit the personnel or
    educational officer to make known to him the educa-
    tional opportunities that could be made available in
    courses related to their particular industry.   Pro-
    cedures should be set up so that the employee would
    receive an authorization form from his employer to
    be submitted to the college at the time of registra-
    tion.

There are several tuition aid plans sponsored by industry:

    a) There are some industries which will pay the
        entire tuition of an employee regardless of
        the kinds of courses he takes.   In this case,
        the employer is generally billed directly by
        the business office of the college.   These com-
        panies will not pay for a course that has to be
        repeated.

    b) Some businesses will completely underwrite
        only those courses which are industry-related.
        In these cases, they pay the entire cost and
        are billed by the college.

    c) It is the policy of some employers to reim-
        burse the employee only when a course is
        completed successfully.   In this situation, the
        college may defer billing the employer until
        these conditions are met.   If the student fails
        to meet this requirement, he is then charged
        for the tuition.

     d)   Other employers will reimburse the employee
on a proportional basis depending on the grades
achieved. These courses may either be in-
dustry-related or nonindustry directed.

The financial aid counselor should be particularly
aware of the overtime factors required of many jobs. In
the case of bank employees who must work overtime during
audit periods, for instance, it is well to advise the student
to take courses later in the evening. Many students have
had to drop early courses because of excessive absences
caused by overtime bank demands. This undoubtedly must
be true of other industries as well. The financial aid
counselor must be aware of these kinds of situations and
advise the student accordingly.

Conclusion

The admission of adult students is of increasing concern to many in higher education. The "open admission"
policies of many colleges have provided an entree into higher education for the recent graduate whose credentials may
include only a high school diploma. Further, the adult student, whose education may have been interrupted for a number of years, must meet rigid academic requirements. This
inequity is aggravated by the lack of financial aid available
to him.

It is essential that loan, grant and scholarship funds
be established for the adult student. The financial aid
counselor must be at the institution at the time the student
is attending. Counseling has to be an integral part of the
financial process. The adult student has every right to expect the best student personnel services possible to enable
him to achieve success in "academe. "

References

1.   Assembly on Goals and Governance, "Assembly Lists
85, Theses to Stimulate Academic Reform" as
reported in The Chronicle of Higher Education,
V, 15, January 18, 1971, p. 5.

2.   Ibid. , p. 5.

3. College Scholarship Service, Manual for financial aid officers, 1970 ed., New York: College Entrance Examination Board, 1970, pp. 4-15, 4-16.

4. Ibid., pp. 4-5.

5. Ibid., pp. 4-6.

6. Ibid., pp. 2-16.

7. Ibid., pp. 5-16.

8. "Ford Foundation to Spend $500,000 Studying Deferred Tuition Idea," The Chronicle of Higher Education, V, 19, February 15, 1971, pp. 1 & 8.

9. Li, P. C., "An Investigation of the Employment Situation of Evening Students - With the Purpose of Helping Them Find Jobs in Their Chosen Fields of Study," in press, Journal of College Placement, October-November 1971 issue.

10. Williams, Beryl W., "University Financial Aid," Proceedings Eleventh Annual Conference, United States Association of Evening Students, (mimeographed), Cleveland, November 1970, Workshop 16.

Chapter VIII

LEGAL COUNSELING

by Jean A. Rockwell

Introduction

Students have "problems. " They are not
necessarily deep-seated disturbances in
the treatment of which a psychologist's
professional skill is required. They are
"problems" because a course of action
that has been undertaken is blocked, and
it is not clear what the student should do
next. The essence is that the individual's
circumstances must be evaluated and a new
course of action formulated. [1]

Counseling services for adults in higher education
have traditionally reflected the counseling services offered
to undergraduate day college students. Although programs
are varied and mirror the unique character of the individual
institution, many do include psychological, financial, and
vocational counseling; testing and placement services and
educational advisement; health services; remedial services;
orientation programs; and a myriad of special services.

This list is meaningful and impressive. Yet, we
may well question whether or not these services are meeting adequately all the needs of today's adult students and
whether or not there are areas in which further services
could and should be offered.

Are there any special "problems" manifested by
adult students which are not covered in our traditional service program? Has our highly industralized and complicated
society created new problems and, therefore, new counseling needs for adult students? Since we have historically
followed the lead of the day college in providing personnel
services for adults, are there any new trends in the day

college which might be adapted to adult students? The answer to these rhetorical questions is--yes! Yes, our adult students do have special problems and counseling needs not met through our current programs. Yes, our technical, legalistic society has created problems which our existing counseling services are not equipped to handle. Yes, there are trends in day colleges which could be adapted to fit the needs of our adult students.

Legal Counseling in Day Colleges

Perhaps one area in which we might follow the lead of day programs is that of legal counseling. Legal counseling services are now being provided for day college students in a variety of colleges sprinkled throughout the United States, but most notably in California. The programs at the University of California, Berkeley, and at California State College, Los Angeles, were reported in detail in the Journal of College Student Personnel, January 1970, and the American Personnel and Guidance Journal, March 1970, respectively. Stanley W. Levy, Director of the Community Counsel Unit, Western Center on Law and Poverty, at the University of Southern California, Los Angeles, commented as follows on the spread of legal counseling on college campuses in California:

> With regard to other campuses which have legal counseling, I recall UCLA, San Fernando Valley State College (Cal State at San Fernando), Cal State at Long Beach and U.C. Santa Barbara. I am sure that by now most of the UC campuses have them, as well as all the Urban State Colleges (such as San Francisco State). [5]

Legal counseling on the California college campuses is concerned with informing students of their legal rights and responsibilities.

> The legal counselor discusses the student's problem with him, provides him with pertinent information and advice, and, if appropriate, refers him to other sources of legal assistance. The integrity of the lawyer-client relationship is preserved at all times, but the legal counselor does not represent the student, arrange bail, or assume an advocate position in court. His function is to provide needed information, help formu-

late a plan to resolve legal difficulties, and in
the process, give needed psychological support. [2]

Who did the legal counseling in these colleges? In
some, members of the campus Law School were consulted
and in some, attorneys outside the institution were used to
avoid possible conflict-of-interest charges.

When legal counseling services were offered at the
University of California, Berkeley, during the 1967-8 school
year, 340 students took advantage of them. "In addition,
about 135 of these had returned at least once; some as many
as five or six times. Thus, in the three quarters, approximately 500 to 550 conferences had been held. "[3] An interesting note is the fact that the majority of these conferences
were emergencies in which the students needed immediate information. What were the types of problems that the legal
advisor encountered?

> The largest single category, 45 per cent, dealt
> with landlord/tenant relations .... Domestic re-
> lations account for 7 per cent .... Accidents
> and injuries were 8 per cent of presented prob-
> lems. The remaining 40 per cent involved other
> areas of the law such as criminal matters; ...
> tax problems; ... contract and debt problems;
> ... housing discrimination; manufacturers' war-
> ranties; immigration, naturalization, and deporta-
> tion; defamation of character and copyright and
> patent. [4]

Older, more mature graduate students tended to consult the
legal counselor more frequently than did their undergraduate,
younger counterparts. Only 19 freshmen consulted the service, as compared to 104 seniors and 122 graduate students.

There were many similarities between the legal counseling program offered at the University of California,
Berkeley, in 1967-1968 and the program offered at the California State College, Los Angeles, in 1968-1969. At California State College, Los Angeles, 302 students took advantage of the service. Approximately half of the questions
received by the legal counselor concerned selective service
(these questions were referred to two special draft counseling programs on campus at the University of California,
Berkeley). The distribution of the remaining cases was as
follows: landlord/tenant, 11. 6 per cent; domestic relations,

9. 6 per cent; contracts, 7. 8 per cent; personal injury, 7
per cent; and criminal law, 6 per cent. At this college,
a follow-up questionnaire was mailed to students who had obtained legal counseling. The questionnaire revealed that 81
per cent of the respondents believed they had received helpful information and that 32 per cent believed they would not
have been able to obtain legal information elsewhere because
of cost or time factors. Students responding to this questionnaire suggested that legal information should be made
available by telephone, that some non-Caucasian lawyers
should be used, and that a booklet of general legal information should be printed.

Legal Counseling for Adult Students

Having seen evidence that legal counseling for day
students can work successfully, let us now turn to the counseling needs of adult evening students in higher education.

The legal counseling programs reported in California
have much in them that could easily be adapted to fit the
needs of adult evening students. Certainly the fact that the
more mature students were those who tended to seek legal
help should have implications for adult guidance programs.
Some of the questions which might be raised concerning the
advisability of offering legal counseling services to adult
students include:

1. Do adults need legal counseling services? In
view solely of the fact that so many problems encountered
by the legal counselors in California tended to deal with
landlord/tenant problems, the answer to this question is
yes. A logical assumption is that adult students are involved in landlord/tenant problems to a greater degree than
are younger day-college students. Adult students also have
a greater need for legal information concerning domestic relations and contracts. Since the adult student in higher education is also a functioning member of society as a whole,
he encounters situations requiring a knowledge of legal in-
tricacies in his everyday life. His need for legal counseling services in many respects thus surpasses the need for
such services evidenced by younger day college students.

2. Would adults use legal counseling services? At
the University of California, Berkeley, more graduate students consulted legal counsel than did freshmen, sophomores,
and juniors put together. The older students used the

service more than did the younger students. According to
Stanley Levy, the attorney connected with the legal counseling program at California State College, Los Angeles, some
evening students did consult with him.

> Yes, evening students did have access to my
> services and a few came in to see me. Most
> evening students had jobs so unless the matter
> was extremely pressing, they did not come in.
> (Some called and I tried to help them over the
> phone.)[6]

Since the legal counselor in this college was only available
during day hours, it is easy to understand why only a few
evening students were able to consult with him in person.
If such services were offered during evening hours, adults
would not have to take time off from their jobs in order to
receive legal counseling. Also, an attorney might be more
available in the evening hours than he would be during day
hours. The evidence indicates that if legal counseling services were provided during evening hours, adult students
would utilize them.

3. Should the university offer such legal counseling
services? There is general agreement that the types of
student personnel services offered by a university should be
determined by the needs of the particular school and its
student body. In this context, legal counseling services
may not be needed by adult students in small suburban colleges which draw exclusively upon middle-class students
having adequate financial resources and accessible legal
services in the community. Also in this context, legal
counseling services are very much needed by adults in
sprawling metropolitan institutions. Such adults, who are
often members of minority groups, frequently do not have
the financial resources nor the time to consult private lawyers concerning their legal problems. Too, many of their
problems are of an emergency nature and they need "just
the facts, Ma'am" fast. If the student service program of
the university is truly based upon a concept of need, many
universities should include legal counseling services as
part of their overall guidance program for adult students.

4. How should a legal counseling program for adults
be implemented? One of the first concerns in setting up a
program of legal counseling for adult students should be
that of insuring that such services are available during

evening hours.   Lawyers who are normally employed to
teach evening classes might be relieved of their teaching
duties and instead employed in the legal counseling program.
If the university has a law school, advice from this source
could be sought.   If the university is adverse to financing
a legal counseling program, its expense might be shouldered
by evening student fees or by the evening student council.
The fees involved in financing legal counseling programs
for adult students should be modest, but should include a
private office for evening use, and a secretary to handle
telephone calls placed during day hours.   It is suggested
that students be encouraged to make appointments, and
that the time of the interview be limited to one-half hour.
The legal counselor should be on duty a minimum of two
nights a week from two to four hours.   Universities in
which a large percentage of adult students are nonwhite
should consider adding appropriate minority group counselors.

If the day college is already providing legal counseling services, the problem is much simpler.   A partial utilization of their services and/or personnel during evening
hours could be arranged with a minimum of expense.

If personnel services are for students, it is only
logical that students should have some voice in the determination of these services.   Universities contemplating offering legal counseling services for adults should attempt to
assess the need for such services by means of a questionnaire to current students.   Certainly those implementing
such services for a trial period should follow the lead of
California State College, Los Angeles, and circulate a follow-up questionnaire to students who had obtained legal
counseling.

Smaller colleges which feel that they cannot institute
a legal counseling program on such a grandiose scale
should consider the printing of a booklet which would con-
tain the answers to frequently asked legal questions.   They
should also make sure that adult students with legal problems are referred to an appropriate agency within the community.

Conclusion

Adult college students have many problems and an
increasingly large number of them are concerned with legal

matters.   Yet, legal counseling for adult students is not
being provided in the majority of our collegiate institutions.
There is a definite need for such services, especially in
large institutions serving a varied student body.   According
to reports from California, when such services are provided,
adult students do use them and do believe that they are very
worthwhile.

These facts indicate that student personnel administrators should evaluate their own guidance programs with a
cold, hard look and attempt to determine whether or not
their institutions might not be those in which the addition
of legal counseling services is indicated.   If the fundamental
purpose of counseling services for adults in higher education is based on a concept of need, programs which do not
include legal counseling can be indicted for failing to achieve
their expressed purpose.   If the general aim of counseling
is to aid the student to gain insight so that he can come to
understand and accept himself and then move in the direction
of greater self-determination and problem solving, then legal
counseling for adult students can play a significant role in
the total university counseling program.   The advancement
of knowledge on all levels is the true purpose of the university, and the transmission of legal information to adult students is consistent with this purpose.

References

1.   Gideonse, Harry D. , "Forward, " in: Siegel, Max,
        ed. , The Counseling of College Students, New York:
        The Free Press, 1968, p. ix.

2.   Kirk, Henry P. and Levy, Stanley W. , "A Lawyer in
        the Counseling Center, " The Personnel and Guidance
        Journal, March 1970, p. 576.

3.   Kirk, Barbara A. , "Legal Counseling for Students, "
        Journal of College Student Personnel, January
        1970, p. 16.

4.   Ibid.

5.   Levy, Stanley W. , letter to J. Rockwell, August 3,
        1970.

Chapter IX

PSYCHOLOGICAL COUNSELING

by Mary T. Howard

This chapter will examine two propositions: first, that the character of our environment is traumatic, and second, that psychological counseling fulfills a demand that can be met rarely through the techniques of operant conditioning.

The ease with which a high rate of success is a-chieved using operant conditioning techniques in modifying human behavior suggests that counselors should carefully assess the desirability of using any other counseling model. [2] The results of the research of Volsky, et al., which indicates that counseled college students do not evidence a decrease in anxiety and defensiveness nor an increase in problem-solving skills is not reassuring. [36] Two decades ago, Eysenck altered therapists to his pessimism about the efficacy of therapeutic intervention. [14] In spite of such evidence, May published a carefully reasoned plea for an escalation of emphasis on psychological counseling. [23] Numerous books and articles continue to be published where the word "relationship" dominates the content and various theoretical models of counseling are examined. [38, 31, 20, 24, 29, 3]

Further, established college and university counseling centers are able to justify staff-size increases on the basis of long lists of students requesting counseling who cannot be accommodated within the man-hours available from existing staff. New colleges employ counselors concurrently with their teaching faculty. Where a desirable ratio of counselors to clients is 1 to 300-400, even using all the psychologists available whether in an applied field or not, a ratio of 1 to 3000-4000 for even school-age clients could not be achieved. That the demand of the public in general is not met by the available applied psychologists is supported by the proliferation of volunteer and community human resource centers. In February of 1971, the American Board on Certification of Counseling Centers, affiliated with the American Personnel and Guidance Association, hosted a meeting designed to review its format and to consider ways of giving official recognition to these community-based agencies offering counseling. Often, the personnel of these agencies are not trained counselors or psychologists; they know little or nothing about counseling models and theory. Yet, the demand for the services of these agencies is sufficient for them to remain open. What is it that they offer that attracts clients?

The primary service the community agencies offer, that which May requested and Schofield noted, many people seem to find it necessary to buy. [23] Schofield referred to it as friendship in the title of his book. [29] Others are referring to the same phenomena when they write about seeking a relationship, acceptance, evidence of self-worth, positive regard, an emotional encounter and/or social contact. [20, 35, 27, 16, 30, 26]

The effects of the technical revolution on industry, manufacturing economics, business production and distribution are not limited to inanimate figures and objects. The life styles of the total population are being disrupted, forced into rapid change, subjected to traumatic decisions that leave people bewildered, confused, anxious, frustrated and irrationally punitive. The demand for counseling, then, is a demand for some temporary shelter in the sandstorm, some stable dependable opportunity for evaluating their conditions, for testing their acceptability, for reassessing the strengths of their coping mechanisms.

The character of the factors that now affect our lives is little different from that which it was 30, 60, or 90 years ago. There were deaths and separation, hunger and illness, friendships and choices, transportation and distribution and riots and wars. What has changed is the speed with which the information about these occurrences reaches each person. When there is a student disturbance in Wisconsin, not only does the student body of that campus know about it right away, but so do the student bodies of all campuses around the country. They not only hear about it, they see it on television, often while it is still occurring. And so often they act upon it themselves. We have learned that events that are geographically distant are now, unlike so many years ago, temporarily close. When a riot occurred

in Detroit in the 1940s, it was usually over before the
people in Kansas City even heard about it. If the riot
were to be repeated in Kansas City, there was ample time
to prepare for it.   The spread of the generalizing effect
was so much slower then.

     Now, events and stimuli bombard us at an ever-in-
creasing pace.   This is not just an age of anxiety; this is
an age of crisis, and "Anxiety is the official emotion of
our age. " (Schlesinger, in Schoonmaker, 1969)[30]   This is
an age where practically every decision is critical and has
immediate, innate effects on the individual and often on a
fair segment of his environment.   The tired Black woman
who refused to move to the back of the bus in the 1950s
did not dream that her action would be one of the forces
that would generate a riot in Watts or a student death or
deaths at Kent State.

     When there is an earthquake in California, friends in
New York can become immediately anxious about the friend
whom they put on a California-bound plane that morning.
The war in Viet Nam is also in one's own living room and
provides the topic for conversation at dinner where the de-
foliation agents can be breathed in with the meat course.

     With such immediacy of information goes immediacy
of decision-making.   Planning for a trip used to be a matter of weeks; an individual's job may now require traveling
on a few hour's notice with all of the attendant decisions
also compressed into this limited time.   Decisions about
moving, taking a new job, divorcing or marrying, obtaining
or exceeding one's credit limitations, attending school or
not, must often be made rapidly.   This immediacy and un-
avoidable involvement produces tension.

     Another source of tension and uncertainty for the in-
dividual is delineated by Goldberg:

> Man has been cast adrift from the traditional an-
> choring institutions of his social system.   In the
> past, venerable, ethical, social and occupational
> concepts and beliefs engendered by institutions,
> served to define the role and function of each
> societal member.   A sense of identity and value
> as a member of society was gained by the indi-
> vidual who was able to internalize these societal
> concepts.   However, the foundations of these

institutions have long been eroding. The stability
of public and private life ... no longer exists. [17]

The author notes that traditional societal institutions,
as we have known them, appear to be collapsing, forcing
individuals to rely on whatever inner resources they may
have. If the social growth and developmental experiences
of the individual, however, have been limited because of
disruptions and inadequacies in his generic family, he has
few resources upon which to draw in strengthening his own
feeling of self-worth and adequacy. The adults of today
grew up during the periods of World War II and the Korean
War with its separated families and distorted role-modeling
of parents. The difficulty of adults in developing appropriate
emotional ties, when their own childhood has not provided
such a model, is demonstrated by Harlow's experiments
with monkeys. When raised without adult models to observe
and with whom they could interact and identify, the infant
monkeys as adults related poorly with other adult monkeys
and rarely reproduced. Directors of orphanages note similar behavior of adults who grew up in institutions.

The increasing popularity of communal living of unrelated family groups; the development of extended family
groups composed of unrelated individuals; attendance at human relations growth laboratories; sensitivity or encounter
groups; and the increasing voluntary use of agencies and centers where various types of counseling for people without
demonstrated pathology is available, all suggest a desperate
search for a satisfying and reasonably stable intense emotional contact. There seem to be efforts to dispel the feelings of alienation and anomie that accompany the rapid deterioration of established social structures and models.
Apparently, the experienced social deprivation evokes a
strong need for social and emotional contact.

Even though behavior modification techniques can
enable a client to reshape some specific maladaptive behavior into a facilitative behavior, and though this change
will probably result in a more satisfying environment, for
a large number of individuals there is no easily definable
specific behavior they wish changed. [19] The reasons most
achieving adults give for seeking counseling are to relieve
feelings of boredom, loneliness and disinterest, or to obtain assistance in making some specific decision that will
have a major effect on their life style. They often know
all of the ramifications of the alternatives but are reluctant

to accept the risks attached to any of the choices.   They
lack confidence in their ability to succeed in a new venture.
Their earlier learning experiences have provided insufficient
opportunities for them to gain confidence; to feel adequate;
to test facilitative coping mechanisms or to experience failure without debilitating emotional trauma.   In a book on the
developmental experiences of pre-school children, Dyrud observes that: "Children who fail a lot are the ones who are
unrealistic about what they think they can do.   Children who
generally succeed have a better idea of what they can do. "[12]
Research studies in the areas of motivation and achievement
support Dyrud's contention.

       The extended families were already a thing of the
past when today's adult population was growing up.   Families were on the move, as much as seven times in their
working lives, and there was neither money to take nor space
to put the grandparents, so the emotional security of an alternate home was not accessible.   Further, there was no
security of stable peer mates since these, too, were left
behind during developmental years.

       So, in spite of the fact that increasing populations
are forcing people into closer and closer physical proximity,
individuals feel very alien and alone and use much of their
energy in defending themselves against perceived possible
emotional injury and concurrently searching for ways to
alleviate the loneliness. [13]

       Psychological counseling involves a relationship be-
tween two people where the content of the communication
revolves consistently around the concerns of the client, his
feelings as reflected in his verbal and nonverbal behavior,
and the effects of his behavior on his relationships as observed in the counseling exchange.   Another way of defining
psychological counseling is that it consists of listening and
talking with an individual about his needs, characteristics
and behaviors which make him similar to or different from
other persons.   In the discussion, particular emphasis is
placed on the rational meaning and emotional implications of
these characteristics.   The purpose of counseling can be
viewed as assisting persons to select goals. [4]   In this definition, the orientation is toward the accomplishment of certain
tasks as defined in the counseling contact.   The concept of
a relationship, however, is implicit in the accomplishment
of the counseling contract.

According to Rogers: "Effective counseling consists of a definitely structured, permissive relationship with allows the client to gain an understanding of himself to a degree which enables him to take positive steps in the light of his new orientation. "[28] "The whole process of counseling should be directed toward helping the client to develop ... positive, self-initiated action. "[28]

Three of the four basic tenets of counseling that Rogers posited four decades ago are directly relevant to the kind of relationship that has as many as one-quarter of the adult population of America are requesting today. [11]

These tenets are:

1. Warmth and responsiveness of counselor which facilitates rapport.

2. Permissiveness in regard to expression of feeling.

3. Development of therapeutic limits, such as rejection of those physically harmful, and adherence to time limits.

4. The counseling relationship is free of any type of pressure or coercion. The counselor does not attempt to impress his own values, wishes, reactions or biases on the client. The counselor does not impose advice on the client. [32]

Psychological counseling requires that the counselor provide an atmosphere that permits the client to make further gains in both maturity and in self-integration. Blocher defines this opportunity for counseling as contributing to development. He considers the counselor as an agent of change who facilitates the development of clients in their social roles, in their developmental tasks and in improving coping behaviors. Levels of human effectiveness in coping behaviors are panic where the individual is emotional and probably completely inefficient in his control of his environment through levels of inertia, striving, coping and mastery. However, where the individual has long-range control over his environment and is active in exerting an effect on it, he then feels adequate. [6] The level of mastery as defined by Blocher is generally not the plane reached by most clients. It is, however, very definitely the level they wish to achieve. "For the counselor in a changing world, it is important to be able to grasp the sweep and magnitude of changes and the intensity with which they will impinge upon the lives of man."[7]

The client needs a nonthreatening, nonjudgmental atmosphere in which he can expose his weaknesses, relax his emotional defenses without fear of the emotional assault common in his everyday experiences. He wants the tempo - rary freedom to dispose of the trappings of the various roles he plays on his job, with his family and friends, in his encounters with strangers. He can then examine himself and selectively and purposefully don whichever trappings he considers adaptive rather than be laden, as many clients tell counselors they are, with a number of behaviors they find inefficient for their goals, but which they have been afraid to defrock because they just might contribute something to the effectiveness of their functioning. One encouraging longitudinal study of college students who had received counseling 25 years earlier, finds that, while the counseled group were still more anxious than the noncounseled group, they were more successful in earning better grades, more honors and degrees, and were even more active in college life. In addition, the counseled group said that they wished there had been more follow-up and that counselors had intervened at crisis points during their college lives. [11]

I have not discussed any of the specific techniques of counseling. These are available from numerous sources. [33, 1, 8, 5, 20, 21, 22, 25, 35, 37, 4, 9, 15, 10, 18] Rather, I have been concerned with the need to encourage recognition of the urgency with which individuals are expressing a demand for nonthreatening opportunities to mature and integrate rapidly enough to cope efficiently with the rapidly increasing bombardment of stimuli generated by the collapse of established modes of behaviors--the increasing pace and numbers of decisions demanded. This is the frightening but yet unacknowledged conflict of feeling as if one were extremely expendable when observing the generalization of effects on others of one's own behavior.

References

1.   Arbuckle, Donald S. , Counseling: Philosophy, Theory and Practice, Boston: Allyn and Bacon, 1965.

2. Bandura, Albert, Principles of Behavior Change, New
   York: Holt, Rinehart and Winston, 1969.

3. Bentley, Joseph C. , The Counselor's Role, Commen-
   tary and Readings, Boston: Houghton Mifflin, 1968.

4. Berdie, Ralph F. , "Counseling Principles and Presump-
   tions, " Journal of Counseling Psychology, Vol. 6,
   Fall 1959, pp. 115-182.

5. Berenson, Bernard G. and Carkhuff, Robert R. , eds. ,
   Sources of Gain in Counseling and Psychotherapy,
   New York: Holt, Rinehart and Winston, 1967.

6. Blocher, Donald H. , Developmental Counseling, New
   York: The Ronald Press, 1966.

7. Ibid. , p. 113.

8. Ibid. , p. 43.

9. Bordin, Edward S. , Diagnosis in Counseling and Psychotherapy, "Readings in Modern Methods of Counseling, "
   Brayfield, A. H. , ed. , New York: Appleton-Century-Crofts, 1950, pp. 102-114.

10. Brammer, Lawrence M. and Shostrom, Everett L. ,
    Therapeutic Psychology: "Fundamentals of Counsel-
    ing and Psychotherapy, " Englewood Cliffs, N. J. :
    Prentice-Hall, 1960.

11. Campbell, David P. , The Results of Counseling:
    Twenty-five Years Later, Philadelphia: W. B.
    Saunders Co. , 1965.

12. Dyrud, Grace, Play to Learn, (c) Grace Dyrud, 1971,
    p. 88.

13. Eldridge, H. Wentworth, "Education in Futurism in
    North America, " The Futurist, Vol. 4, No. 5
    December 1970, pp. 193-196.

14. Eysenck, H. J. , "The Effects of Psychotherapy: An
    Evaluation, " Journal of Consulting Psychotherapy,
    Vol. 16, 1952, pp. 319-324.

15. Gelso, Charles J. , "Different Worlds: A Paradox in Counseling and Psychotherapy, " Journal of Counseling Psychotherapy, " Vol. 17, No. 3, May 1970, pp. 271-278.

16. Goldberg, Carl, Encounter: Group Sensitivity Training Experience, New York: Science House, 1970.

17. Ibid. , pp. 21-22.

18. Gustad, J. W. , "The Evaluation Interview in Vocational Counseling, " Personnel and Guidance Journal, 1957, vol. 36, pp. 242-250.

19. Howard, Mary T. , "The Meaning and Potency of Verbal Reinforcers for Psychiatric Patients, " Proceedings of the 76th Annual Convention of the American Psychological Association, 1968, pp. 3-4.

20. Kell, Bill L. and Mueller, William J. , Impact and Change: A Study of Counseling Relationships, New York: Appleton-Century-Crofts, 1966.

21. Krumboltz, John D. , "Behavioral Goals for Counseling, " Journal of Counseling Psychology, vol. 13, Summer 1966, pp. 153-159.

22. Lofquist, Lloyd H. , "An Operational Definition of Rehabilitation Counseling, " in: Patterson, C. H. , ed. , Counseling as a Relationship: Readings in Rehabilitation Counseling, Champaign, Ill. : Stipes Pub. Co. , 1960, pp. 117-121.

23. May, Eugene P. , "Quantity or Quality in Dealing with Human Problems, " Personnel and Guidance Journal, January 1971, vol. 49, no. 5, pp. 376-382.

24. Overholt, William A. , Some Observations on Student Personnel Practice in Selected Overseas Universities (c) 1965, Library of Congress Catalog Card No. 65-29321.

25. Patterson, C. H. , ed. , Counseling as a Relationship: Readings in Rehabilitation Counseling: Champaign, Ill. : Stipes Pub. Co. , 1960, pp. 122-125.

26. Reading Book: Laboratories in Human Relations

Training, rev. 1970, NTL Institute for Applied
Behavioral Science.

27. Rogers, Carl R., Counseling and Psychotherapy, Cam-
     bridge, Mass.: Riverside Press, 1942.

28. Ibid., p. 18.

29. Schofield, William, The Purchase of Friendship,
     Englewood Cliffs, N. J.: Prentice-Hall, 1964.

30. Schoonmaker, Alan N., "Anxiety and The Executive,"
     American Management Association, Inc., 1969.

31. Strong, Stanley R. and Schmidt, Lyle D., "Trust-
     worthiness and Influence in Counseling," Journal
     of Counseling Psychology, vol. 17, No. 3, May
     1970, pp. 197-204.

32. "Student Life Characteristics," Counseling Center
     Report, Washington, D. C.: Federal City College,
     1971.

33. Sundberg, Norman D. and Tyler, Leona A., Clinical
     Psychology, New York: Appleton-Century-Crofts,
     1962.

34. Super, D. E., "Transition from Vocational Guidance
     to Counseling Psychology," Journal of Counseling
     Psychology, 1955, vol. 2, pp. 3-9.

35. Tyler, Leona E., The Work of the Counselor, New
     York: Appleton-Century-Crofts, 1969.

36. Volsky, Theodore; McGoon, Thomas M.; Norman,
     Warren T. and Hoyt, Donald P., The Outcomes
     of Counseling and Psychotherapy: Theory and Re-
     search, University of Minnesota Press, Minnea-
     polis, Minnesota, 1965.

37. Vosbeck, Phyllis D., "An Exploratory Study of the
     Effects of Counseling," unpublished Master's thesis,
     University of Minnesota, 1959.

38. Weschler, Irving R. and Schein, Edgar H., "Issues

in Human Relations Training (Five), " National
Training Laboratories, National Education Association, Washington, D. C. , 1962.

Chapter **X**

COUNSELING ADULTS THROUGH
EXTRA-CURRICULAR ACTIVITIES

by Jerrold L Hirsch

> ... club activities, guided by wise and under-
> standing persons, can turn into desired per-
> sonal strengths in those who belong... [1]

In today's society, group life is essential. Free association is, in a real sense, the measure for the freedom
of a country. Only where the total community participates
in the creation of its culture and of its mores are free expression and free communication encouraged or permitted.

This is not the fact in countries organized around a
figure representing the dominating role. A democratic society imposes a shared responsibility upon each of its citizens. It also offers a share of the gains that accrue.
Such a society considers its citizens mature and capable of
reflection, self-direction, and group participation.

A political oligarchy, on the other hand, treats the
population as though they were infants. Aside from the fact
that economic interests and mass exploitation are always
motives behind such a scheme, the assumption of an auto-
cratic regime is that the population is incapable of understanding and reflection; that its will is capricious and un-
reliable, and therefore, needs to be diverted and repressed.
The dependence of early childhood upon the judgment and authority of elders and/or the powerful is perpetuated as a
government practice.

The success of a democracy rests upon the individual's capacity of self-determination and voluntary group life.
Freedom in group life is a relationship in which only the
most mature can participate fully. A democracy is posi-
sible only to the degree that the maturity of its citizens
permits. Childish dependence, ambition, and self-centered-

ness in the adult make cooperative effort and group integration impossible. Accordingly, group education in a democratic plan of life has two major functions to perform. In the first place, it must direct the orderly and wholesome development of the personality. Its second major duty is to develop those dispositions of man's nature that make him desirous and capable of participating in a progressive and evolving society.

In counseling the adult student through extra-curricular activities, the insularity of the small group must expand to include the affairs of the world. The feeling of responsibility will extend to include the neighborhood, the community and the world. Education's aim is to direct social impulses into "political action" for social betterment.

There are many individuals, especially adults, who lack the essential patterns of behavior in a group relationship; they do not possess elementary cultural tools for group life. These are individual students; adults who have not acquired even rudimentary social values. They hardly take cognizance of the needs and conveniences of others. These individuals have to be re-educated. They must learn the simplest concepts and practices of human relationships. Group experience with a purpose and wholehearted interest is perhaps the most certain method of reaching such individuals, for they learn by experience as well as through abstract teaching. The activity, student government, the student newspaper, professional and vocational organizations, special interest clubs; also, "institutional activities" such as concerts, lectures, films, and committees on educational change and community involvement must supply the face-to-face contact in an informal relationship where the conflicts, hostilities, friendships and cooperation can occur and find expression. It is common knowledge that personality is altered through interaction and firsthand experience.

A great part of important education is derived from group experience, human relationships and, in essense, through extra-curricular activities. Whether it is learning facts or skills, training of character, or development of personality, the educative process is a social one. It occurs either in the family, the classroom, the clique, the club, or other such temporary or permanent groups. The important fact that must be noted is that the group experiences tending to improve human beings most effectively are

those that bring the individual more closely into human relationships with his contemporaries.

Student activities, extra-curricular or co-curricular
activities, therefore, permit the operation of indirect influences, largely through the interplay of individuals involved,
the students, the adviser, and the counselor. In this experience, the materials are the emotional conflicts and har-
monies, identification with one another, and the interaction
of ideas. The process here is the process of togetherness
through realistic and actual experience under the guidance
of an empathetic and sensitive counselor. Indeed, this is
dedication and professionalism! To be accepted, to have love
and gratification, is one of our basic needs. Cogent group
experiences and education must supply this. In addition, it
is clear that to give satisfaction to the individual member
and to enhance his feelings of self-esteem and work are para-
mount. Therefore, these activities must include creative
work for the individual as well as for the group, with shared
responsibility, for its value lies in its capacity to release
creative individuals as well as social drives.

Another major value is the socializing effect. All
satisfaction derived from relationships with people, from
self-esteem, and from creative work disposes one toward
establishing social attitudes. A person whose love and
friendships are satisfactory, who receives adequate recognition, and who is successful in his work tends to be constructive in his group and personal relations.

Adult groups enjoying the guidance of a professional
can be extremely efficient and reliable in proposing ideas,
making mutual decisions, and promoting projects. The
group has a vast potential if students and counselors are
aware of the techniques of improving the quality of the activities. Group activities should provide a variety of experiences to meet the needs of all and should foster student initiative.

The following remarks made by adults attending the
evening division of Staten Island Community College empha-
size the benefits and changes made in their attitudes and
values during and after their involvement in extra-curricular activities in the evening division of the college.

It was purely by accident that I became involved
in student activities; most of my time and energy

was being spent at work, at home with the family, rushing through my courses at night and paying little attention to outside activities.

I got involved looking for escape and instead I found the ability to deal with myself and my problems.

I want to feel that I am contributing in improving our society and student activities provides me with this means.

Reflecting back, the Activities Counselor gave me much more than I was looking for.

Through activities I have matured and now can accept criticism. I feel I am able to a greater degree to communicate with my friends. I did not at first realize that the more I got involved, the easier it would be to relate to those around me.

I gained a new sense of responsibility and that responsibility grew with involvement.

The most important outcome of my involvement in student activities is the drastic change in my outlook on school, life, and my role in the community.

I have changed my views on the value of my education, in facing everyday life and the problems of our times.

... [Counseling] made me more aware of the role of the university not only as a classroom but as a place where ideas are exchanged, programs initiated, policies formed, and problems tackled through group communication.

I began to realize how much I had been missing by not being involved personally. My experience until then had been one of noninvolvement--both in and out of class. My outlook on life and my education began to change as a result of extracurricular experiences.

My appreciation and my respect for the people I
saw around me began to grow.

I can now appreciate the need for student involvement, for extracurricular activities, and the need
for an adviser. I can see the value of having
groups work together, the need for students to
diversify their academic activities and not concentrate solely on pursuing sometimes misguided academic goals.

Counseling, a basic need of man, is something which
is sought consciously or unconsciously from youth to age.
We must always be following a path and we will be guided,
whether by chance or by design. The guidance of circum-
stances--the opportune, the immediate--can lead to a good
and rewarding life, but it also can lead, and too often does,
to a life of aimless effort, wasted talents and lost opportunities.

As one grows, he is subject to the unconscious guidance which comes from the influence of the world around us.
As the educational program becomes more diversified and
complex, adult students are faced with decision and choices
which must be made in terms of their own personalities, activities, skill and potentialities.

According to Goldie R. Kaback.

... [T]he counselor in student personnel work
with adults begins with a belief in man's ability
to grow and to change. He hopes that the counseling relationship will help the client to:
1. discover how to actualize his potentialities;
2. develop capacities to respond to new experi-
   encies; and
3. learn to integrate such experiences into a
   meaningful confident pattern of life which is
   congruent with the deeper value of his society. [2]

Through my experiences in encouraging the development of such extra-curricular programs for adults, I sub-
mit that the role of counselor, as Goldie R. Kaback states,
is the major determinant in the process. [3]

A counselor working in student activities with adults,

must gain sufficient insight into the understanding of the
adult behavior so that the needs of the adults and adult
groups can be identifiable. As counselor in student activities for adults, a continuous process of evaluation of one-
self as a person and as an advisor and counselor must be
maintained. Goals are the motivating force behind determining which techniques and resources are used and, hopefully,
the individuals determine the activity.

In conclusion, a remark by Reuben R. McDaniel, Jr. :

> If we are to be educators rather than managers,
> and if we are to make a difference in our institu-
> tions in terms of the educational experiences that
> adults are having, and if we believe that the edu-
> cational process in which the adult is engaging is
> really a way of life, then I think that we can be
> instrumental in the development of meaningful and
> relevant objectives for the co-curriculum activities
> program. [4]

References

1. Fedder, Ruth, ed. , Guidance Through Club Activities;
Lloyd-Jones, Esther, "Foreword," New York:
Columbia University Teachers College Press, 1965.

2. Kabakc, Goldie R. , "Implications for Counseling the
Adult, " in: Thompson, Clarence H. , ed. , Counsel-
ing the Adult Student, Washington, D. C. : American
College Personnel Association, 1967, p. 20.

3. Ibid. , p. 14.

4. McDaniel, Reuben, R. , Jr. , "The Counselor and Co-
Curricular Activities for Adults, " in: Clarence H. ,
ed. , College Personnel Services for the Adult,
Washington, D. C. , American College Personnel
Association, 1968, p. 44.

Chapter XI

COUNSELING MINORITY GROUP ADULTS IN HIGHER EDUCATION

by Eleanor Young Alsbrook

The words in the title of this chapter could have different meanings to different people; thus, the author feels that a clarification of whom and what she is talking about, is necessary at the very beginning.

Counseling: Assisting or helping minority
                         adults make wise decisions con-
                         cerning their educational, voca-
                         tional and personal lives.

Minority Group Adult: Blacks were chosen as the group
                         because the author is more famil-
                         iar with Blacks than any other
                         minority group.

Higher Education: Education beyond high school, in
                         a college or university setting.

The references at the end of this chapter, by and about Blacks, is a suggested list of books for counselors of Black students.

Minority Group Adults and Higher Education

If Black adults are to aspire to the equal opportunity concept, they must be given the opportunity to obtain the academic credentials that are needed to compete in today's society. A number of reports show that less than 2 per cent of the students in major state universities are Black. Too few schools are making an honest attempt to recruit Black students. Evening colleges appear to be doing even less recruiting than day schools. There seems to be even less sincere efforts being placed on retention of Black adult

students once they are enrolled in evening colleges.   Few
and limited tutorial programs, remedial classes or make-
up courses are provided by the administrators of evening
schools.   There is considerable fear of lowering standards
in predominately white institutions with too little consideration given to past discrimination against Blacks.   Some Black
adults are deprived of higher education because of admission
standards that do not take into account the inferior schools
of the slums.

Most American colleges and universities provide personnel and programs to help guide foreign students through
the institution to the completion of their goals.   The same
type of counseling assistance should be provided for Black
students pursuing American higher education.

Minority Group Adult Life Style

There are all types of Black adults pursuing or considering entering higher education.   Some of these are self-
sufficient adults who know what they want and know how to
go about achieving their objectives.   They usually have financial, family and inner security.   They may need no more
than the regular counseling program.

Another type is the younger adult who has been deprived and outwardly resents this fact.   He is not afraid to
ask for guidance or help, though he may not be aware of all
the opportunities that the university provides or should provide to help him to accomplish his goals.   This group is
willing to discuss the shortcomings of the university when
given the opportunity to do so.   They are also willing to
help make the university a meaningful institution for all
the students and a worthwhile school of learning for the entire community.

Still another life style is that of the older, fright-
ened and low-income student.   He seeks higher education to
escape the low-income trap by which he has been surrounded.
These adults are generally shy and afraid to ask questions
for fear of appearing stupid.   Unless these individuals have
exceptionally good counselors who will give them a great
deal of individual attention, they could quit college at any
point and blame themselves, even though they may have a
high potential in academic learning.

Most of the above types of Black adult students have

some of the following fears: not being accepted; being over-
tested; not being understood by teachers because of communication problems; not passing; not feeling a part of the institution; not being wanted; being talked down to; experiencing an
educational gap between themselves and students with better
educational backgrounds; and poor health.   In addition, they
may suffer from (or think they suffer from): poor writing
ability; lack of reading techniques; incomplete financial support or not getting better paid jobs so that they can take care
of their families while going to school; and not being able to
receive free tutoring in order to keep up with their classes.

Communication is the important gap between Blacks
and Whites.   Most Black adults entering evening colleges
have a distinct Black language and Black culture.   Most university teachers do not make allowances for these differences.
Some Black adult students have problems interpreting the
teacher's questions, just as some teachers have difficulty
interpreting the Black student's answers.   Yet the Black student is the one who suffers from this communication gap.
Black students should be able to make appointments with
their teachers in the evening to discuss these communication
problems.

There should be more qualified counselors available
in the evening so that Black adult students could use their
services.   These counselors could help the Black adult students to cope with some of the problems mentioned, which
could determine whether or not these students complete their
goals.

Counselors for Minority Group Adult Students

Counselors for Black adult students, whether Black
or White, should be patient, pleasant and understanding.
Above all, they should be unfailingly perceptive and intuitive
in relating to the student's particular problems.

Black adults are looking for someone who knows how
to make them feel comfortable and at ease.   Counselors for
Black adults should be able to interpret the Black language
of the ghetto with empathy for the students.   These students
want to be accepted and understood by the counselor, but not
with condescension or paternalism.   Black adult students do
not care to listen to the counselor hedge or to find their
needs unrecognized.   They, like other adults, need the
counselor to do some exploration for them--in some cases

by merely using the telephone to obtain answers.

Counselors of Black students should have enough time to spend with these adults so that they will not feel that the interview has been overly hurried. Some of them are especially sensitive, fearful, distrustful, and watchful of any hint of doubt in the counselor's attitude. The doubt in the Black student's mind may come from the abuse that the Blacks have experienced in the past. Thus, the counselor must be honest, patient, sincere at all times and truly care about the student.

There should be both Black and White counselors on staffs where there is an integrated student body. At least this gives the student a chance to select the counselor with whom he can best communicate. This also gives the counselors an opportunity to refer the students that they feel they cannot reach to other counselors. Most advisers feel that they can help all students, without realizing that some counselees are not able to respond to their method of counseling.

The counselors should be good listeners who carefully analyze and relate to what the students are saying. They should be competent in identifying conflicts and encouraging self-analysis. It is so easy for counselors to take over the conversation when students are having difficulties in expressing themselves. Moreover, the counselor must understand that the student's ego and his self-concept are all-important.

Some Black adults want to be offered exactly that for which they ask. If they want facts, they should be given facts; if they want suggestions, they should be given suggestions with alternatives. Some Black adult students are resentful at what they call "beating around the bush. "

Counselors working with Black adults should have some insight into the Black person's culture which can be achieved by reading books by and about Blacks and by visiting Blacks in the Black neighborhood.

For counselors to be truly sensitive to the Black student's feelings, they should arrange to be in encounter groups with Blacks, especially with those who have been deprived and are not too middle-class to "tell it how it is. "

A counselor for Black adult students should secure

the following information during the first counseling session:

1. Does the counselee appear to be a secure or an insecure person?

2. Does he know what he wants from the institution?

3. Does he have short-range or long-range goals?

4. Do his goals seem realistic according to his conversation, in light of past education, job experience, test scores, family situation, recommendation, and the counselor's observation?

5. Does he appear well-informed about his goals and the direction to be taken?

6. Does he appear capable of performing independently or will there be need for continued assistance such as tutoring?

7. Does he need remedial, vocational, financial or emotional help?

8. Does he need perceptive teachers who will arrange enough conference time to insure understanding of course requirements?

9. Does he have health problems that could be corrected if given the proper attention, or if money were available for this purpose?

10. Does he appear self-confident or is supportive help needed?

All the above, of course, holds true should the counselee be an adult female student.

Techniques of Counseling Minority Group Adult Students

There may be some similarities in counseling minority group adults with counseling any other group of students. Thus, it is hoped that anyone reading this chapter will find cogent techniques that may prove useful.

Counseling techniques that should be expected of all students of Black adult students are:

1. Reflection of feelings
2. Reassurance
3. Clarification
4. Interpretation
5. Information-giving
6. Advice and suggestion-giving
7. Question-answering
8. Coping with resistance
9. Coping with defense mechanism
10. Handling hostility
11. Encountering transference
12. Contend with dependency
13. Coping with misunderstanding and mis-interpretation
14. Continuous and frequent follow-up methods

The rest of this section will be devoted to techniques to be used from the time Black students enter school until the time they complete their goals.

Upon entering college, Black students should be put into a large group-counseling session or group-guidance meeting. The purpose for this gathering is to let the adults see a number of other people that find themselves in the same situation; namely, beginning their education at an older age. In the large group session, shy individuals do not feel singled out or inferior as they might be if being counseled for the first time individually. They also hear others ask questions that they would have been perturbed to ask. This large group should not be for Blacks only. To the contrary, it should be a common meeting for all entering adult students.

The leader should have a personable appearance and have a feeling for words which includes that particular talent of being able to put people at their ease, never overlooking the fact of speaking slowly and distinctly.

The first order of business should be a cordial, warm and sincere welcome to the university. The counselor should make it plain that she understands the fears and anxieties of entering students. They should be told that counselors either have been or will be assigned to them to aid in any problems which may arise.

Each adult student should be issued a catalog and a handbook. The group leader should explain each section of and a question period should follow in which the answers should be succinct and clarifying.

The second technique should entail the breaking down
of the large group into various small groups.   Each leader
of the small groups should hand out complete registration
forms and explain these forms most carefully.   A trial registration could then be attempted.   A tour of the campus would
assist the students not only to find their classrooms more
easily but would give them a further sense of belonging.

This type of special catering may not be necessary
for all adults, but it is needed and desired by adults from
the deprived sections of the community.

The last technique is to finalize the assignment of a
counselor to each student.   The student should be told where
the counselor's office is and then, most importantly, the
counselor should set up an appointment with his counselee
immediately in order to guarantee him an auspicious start.
At the end of the first counseling appointment, a second appointment should be allocated to convince the students that
there is a genuine and sincere desire to help them.   Continuous counseling should be given until the students have
completed their goals.

Conclusion

I would like to re-emphasize the need for more qualified counselors of Black adult students in higher education.
The main qualification of the counselors should be the sincere desire to see these minority group adults complete
their original goals.

Counselors for minority groups should be carefully
chosen.   They should be extremely patient, highly personable,
completely honest and very knowledgeable about the oppres-
sion of minority groups.   The counselors of these groups
should be able to overlook hostility, distrust and nonaccept-
ance and by so doing, create an atmosphere of confidence,
trust, mutual understanding and open communication.

In this chapter, it was stated that Black counselors
should be on the counseling staff.   This should not be con-
strued to mean that all Black counselors should be assigned
to all Black students since some Black counselors, just like
some White counselors, are not emotionally equipped to counsel minority adult students.

As was mentioned in this chapter, group and individual counseling are needed for minority adults. Follow-up counseling is a prime necessity even if the student does not continue to ask for help. Counseling for these students must be continuous from their first week to their completion of school.

My recommendations for counseling minority group adults in higher education are:

1. Special counseling programs should be developed for minority group adults which provide for their unique needs. This program should be evaluated at the end of each semester and records kept on an on-going basis.

2. Counselors should be employed who have the special qualifications and skills necessary to work effectively with these adults.

3. Records should be kept of the successful counseling of minority group adults. The techniques and methods used to achieve success should be shared with other institutions of higher learning.

References

1. Bennett, Lerone, Before the Mayflower, Chicago: Science Research Associates, 1969.

2. Billingsley, Andrew, Black Families in White America, Englewood Cliffs, N. J. : Prentice-Hall, 1968.

3. Clark, Kenneth, Prejudice and Your Child, Boston: Beacon Press, 1955.

4. Drotning, Phillip T. and South, Wesley, Up from the Ghetto, New York: Cowles Book Co. , 1970.

5. Franklin, John Hope, From Slavery to Freedom, New York: Knopf, 1967.

6. Gladwin, Thomas, Poverty, U. S. A. , Boston: Little, Brown, 1967.

7. Gordon, Edmund W. and Wilkerson, Dozey A. , Compensatory Education for the Disadvantaged, New

York: College Entrance Examination Board, 1966.

8.   Guthrie, Robert V. , Being Black: Psychological-
     Sociological Dilemma, New York: Harper and Row,
     1970.

9.   Jordon, Winthrop, White Over Black: American Atti-
     tudes Toward the Negro 1550-1812, Chapel Hill:
     University of North Carolina Press, 1968.

10. Katz, S. , ed. , Negro and Jew, New York: Mac-
     millan, 1967.

11. Krech, David, Crutchfield, R. S. , and Ballochey, E.
     L. , Individual and Society, New York: McGraw-
     Hill, 1962.

12. King, Martin Luther, Jr. , Why Can't We Wait?, New
     York: New American Library, 1964.

13. Malcolm X, The Autobiography of Malcom X, New
     York: Grove Press, 1965.

14. Marx, G. T. , Protest and Prejudice, New York:
     Harper, 1967.

15. Parsons, Talcott and Clark, Kenneth B. , The Negro
     American, Boston: Beacon Press, 1967.

16. Nash, Gary B. and Weiss, Richard, The Great Fear:
     Race in the Mind of America, New York: Holt,
     Rinehart & Winston, 1970.

17. Pervin, Lawrence A. and Reik, Louis E. and Dalrymple,
     Willard, eds. , The College Dropout and the Utiliza-
     tion of Talent, Los Angeles: Western Psychological
     Services, 1970.

18. Yinger, Milton J. , A Minority Group in American
     Society, New York: McGraw-Hill, 1965.

19. Young, Whitney M. Jr. , Beyond Racism, New York:
     McGraw-Hill, 1969.

Chapter XII

WHITE STUDENTS IN A BLACK COLLEGE

by Beryl Warner Williams

Introduction:
Developing an Awareness of the White Minority

The matter of race as it irritates or stimulates the relationships of the black and white people in the United States has taken on various interpretations. Some explain by historical fiction or by autobiography what it means to be black in a white society as does Margaret Walker in Jubilee, or Vivian Washington in Mount Ascutney. Others try to determine white alliance with the black society as does John Howard in Black Like Me or Melissa Mather in One Summer in Between or Martin Luther King, Jr., in Where Do We Go From Here or Whitney M. Young, Jr., in Beyond Racism.

Statistics on the comparative growth of racial groups in American cities, however, have not really elicited a frank or scientific appraisal of a society where black is predominant, particularly where the white may wish to remain or return to black educational facilities to develop his potential. Such a lack has prompted this presentation--some approaches to the problem of counseling white students in a black college. The thousands of administrators, teachers, or counselors, white or black, in the predominantly black college have been involved in this aspect of counseling for over a hundred years.

Morgan State College, a predominantly black college founded in 1867, has had white students in classes from its inception as the Centenary Biblical Institute and many another black college has had the same situation, indicates its register emeritus, Edward N. Wilson, as he reminisces from facts stored in his mind. The outcomes, whether satisfactory or not, have not been recorded. This writer, who is not a professional counselor, challengers all who

work with adults, particularly white students in the predominantly black college, to record such helpful information.   A-
wareness of current aspects of this problem is now presented
from the experiences of a black administrator in a predominantly black college.

    After seven years of developing the coordinated pro-
gram of the evening and summer sessions at Morgan State
College, I am prepared for the hesitant, sometimes belliger-
ent, voice at the other end of the telephone line:

> Do you have an evening school out there?
>
> Since Morgan is near by home and would save the
> time of going to a college in the country at night,
> I would like to come over there.   Do you accept
> whites?
>
> Do you accept evening graduates of high schools?
> How about evening graduates of community colleges?
>
> My daughter (son) was a good student in the ad-
> vanced preparatory course of a local high school.
> She (he) had an unfortunate situation.   Can she (he)
> register for biology at night?
>
> My college does not have sufficient summer courses
> in education (history, psychology, sociology, etc.).
> Could I take courses at Morgan State in the summer
> evenings to complete my requirements?
>
> (Long distance:)
> I am a student in California (Ohio, Utah, Florida,
> etc.) and shall be home in Baltimore this summer.
> Could I enroll in black studies at Morgan?
>
> Can I qualify for a state teaching certificate by tak-
> ing courses at Morgan?   I've been a teacher for 32
> years.   I have in-service credits?
>
> Is your college accredited?   Can I transfer credits
> from the night school at Morgan to the community
> college?
>
> Is your school under the state system of colleges?
> Can I transfer credits to the university?

How can a night school student get scholarships or
loans at Morgan?   I'm white.

Can you accept credits from ---- (nonaccredited
business or professional school, G. I. vocational
institute, etc.).   Why not?   I know that other colleges do not accept the credits, but I thought ....
I paid a thousand dollars for that work.

What high school courses do you offer?

So go the questions, by telephone for the most part,
but sometimes in face-to-face counseling.   There may be a
long-haired male, 17 years old, or a 57-year old weary,
white teacher of long public school experience.   They would
be but two among the nonblacks who may become part of the
15 per cent of the undergraduate evening students or the 48
per cent of the graduate students who inquire and enter the
college program.   How can we know such a percentage?

Within the past seven years, the earlier custom of
protest over identifying students by race has suddenly changed.
Federal insistence on compliance in integration has caused
higher education to identify students of races other than the
predominant one (whether predominant means white or black).
Federal grants and foundation grants have been built into
their proposals that there must be aid to and facilities for
students without regard to race.   Since application blanks,
registration cards, and various data-processed cards have
no identifying letter or punched area, persons who conduct
registration now may go through a simple face-to-face count
to provide the necessary information on the relative percentage of races.   Registration by mail affects this accuracy.
At one time, location of home, nature of job, name of high
school and possibly name of registrant could identify the students as nonblack.   In the rapid changes in neighborhoods
and the increases in job opportunities, such stereotyped i-
dentification is less and less possible.   Neither is voice
quality a real cue by telephone.   Very infrequently, the white
student will mention the name of a white faculty member on
campus.   Hence, counseling the white student has resulted
in observations on his model on campus, the white teacher.

White Minority in a Black College Faculty

Morgan State College has long been cited as an integrated college in administration and faculty.   For the first

72 years, the presidents were white and many early white
faculty members in the Methodist traditions were so-called
educational missionaries intent on educating black children
and adults. As previously mentioned from the reminiscenses
of the registrar emeritus, some faculty members attended
classes with the black students and encouraged a few white
adults in the community to do so, many years ago.

At present, the college has an appreciable percentage
of non-Black faculty. By actual count in the current college
catalog, 23 per cent are non-Negro (including American Indians, East Indians, Pakistanis, Chinese and displaced Euro-
peans).

Reasons for non-Blacks teaching at Morgan State College are reported as follows:

1. The college as a state institution has a policy
    of racial integration, accepting qualified faculty
    of any race.

2. Experience at Morgan State College enhances
    one's availability in the great search for white
    teachers who have had experience teaching in
    black schools.

3. The universities in the Baltimore area turning
    out a high number of Ph. D. 's, many of whom
    have had years of teaching experience.

4. Baltimore provides an opportunity for going to
    graduate school while teaching, although this
    is moonlighting in another college, particularly
    the community college.

5. Business and industry also attract white teach-
    ers and consultants to a second (part-time)
    job.

6. Salaries at Morgan State College are competi-
    tive, according to the scale for all state col-
    leges, especially for the very young white teach-
    er on the way up, or the older or even retired
    white teacher who may be writing, following an
    ideal, or just resting.

7. White teachers avoid the compulsion of serving

on committees in addition to teaching, especially if blacks fail to appoint or elect them to
committees.

8. Some white teachers, beyond any of the above,
    have the love of teaching almost to the exclu-
    sion of any naturalistic factors.

The image of the white teacher as model, consultant,
even friend is not clear.

White Minority in a Black Student Body

For over 20 years, because of its student body,
Morgan State College has been publicized as a radically integrated institution. In the modern sense, reasons for white
student attendance were quite utilitarian. White students at
Morgan State in the 1950s were often the well-meaning liber-
als misunderstood in other colleges, the social misfits, the
youths alienated from family, or the overseas white who
hoped to overcome his language barrier. These sought
either a refuge, an escape or a place to regain a feeling
of security or even superiority.

One break-through for leadership in integration at
Morgan State came with the Ford Foundation-supported Institute for Political Education. Mock political conventions with
visiting white colleges, politicians and the flash of newspaper
publicity gave the college a new dimension of dignity and responsibility to the public scene. White students came on a
kind of "exchange" procedure to study in the Institute. The
League of Women Voters gave advice and white politicians
came to observe evidences of the growing power of the black
vote. In a few instances, some of the white adults became
part-time students, auditing courses or taking them for credit.

In the early 1960s, the experience with racially integrated high schools in the Baltimore area encouraged white
students to attend Morgan. The difficulty of getting into the
larger colleges and the rising costs of tuition made this
state-supported college, with its almost open-door policy
and its lower costs, attractive. The civil rights movement
contributed to the interest of white students in black students;
their problems and their colleges.

Student Personnel Services at Morgan State College

sent both counseling staff and faculty members to predominantly white high schools to reassure all students that they were welcome.   In spite of advance counseling by white counselors, who advised white students not to attend Morgan State, the number of white students increased, though at a small rate.   White students who previously often came on campus only to attend classes, began to be visible in the choir, the R. O. T. C. , the football team, and other student activities.   Students at nearby four-year colleges and the community colleges came to register as special students at night while attending their other colleges during the day.   In some instances, these transferred to Morgan State as night students to complete requirements for a bachelor's degree while they worked during the day.

The latter half of the 1960s saw several developments. Morgan State became part of the state system of colleges functioning under a single board of trustees.   Reciprocal programs of allowing students to attend classes at any of the state colleges in the area led to greater participation of white students.   Meetings of administrators, faculty, and students developed interest and set some policies.   Private colleges in the area also exchanged students who wanted black studies or summer courses in languages not otherwise available.   The pressure of federal legislation to withhold funds from segregated schools led eventually in Maryland to the hiring of personnel to see that state colleges were actually integrated.   Morgan State thus acquired a white coordinator of integration, operating out of counseling services. The new coordinator made visits to public schools in the city and county, planned joint television and radio spots with Coppin State in Baltimore (also predominantly black), with Towson State in the county, and with the University of Maryland, Baltimore County campus (predominantly white), to show that neither black nor white was the color of any of these four state-supported institutions in metropolitan Baltimore.

In 1968 and 1969, strong interest in black power and black awareness made both black and white students at Morgan State reassess their college attendance.   A vocal minority of black students, spurred on by visits of Malcolm X, Muhammad Ali, Dick Gregory, Stokely Carmichael, and Rap Brown over a five-year period, declared the college was for blacks.   The retiring president, through the news media, reaffirmed the college as racially integrated.   Nevertheless, white students enrolled in an informal visiting exchange such as that with Colby Junior College in New England and Hood College in a northern Maryland county, despite the belligerence of some black students, have increased in number during the past three years. Black and white faculty from each of the schools have been involved in short-term exchanges from a day to a week in length. Other projects such as the University of Pennsylvania-Morgan student exchange and single students from Amherst and other colleges have attracted additional white students.

White Students in an Evening Program

Against this summary of observations on whites in a black college are projected programs of the evening and summer and extension sessions at Morgan State College. By visual count over the past few years, the number of white students in the evening program has increased from approximately 2 per cent to 15 per cent, never approaching, however, as many as 100 students. White students today have these reasons for attending Morgan State:

1. anxiety to avoid the draft;
2. interest in black studies program;
3. transfer to Morgan from a college farther away;
4. acquiring transferable credits for professional training as a nurse, medical lab assistant, physical therapist;
5. updating or completing qualifications for teaching;
6. curiosity about a black college;
7. completing requirements for a degree in a smaller college;
8. being encouraged to go to college or to return to college by a black friend on the job;
9. interest in the urban studies program; and
10. opportunities for independent study.

The development of an evening student council in the past four years has been discovered as a means not only for white students to become a part of and to contribute to the college program but to serve as council officers and leaders as well. Three white students in the past three years have held office and others have travelled with black council members to regional and national evening student gatherings at colleges in New York, Pennsylvania, District of Columbia, Maryland and Virginia. They have observed black students in the minority at the larger colleges. They have discovered that interests and problems of evening students are not necessarily classified by the color of the student, or the location or size of the college.

Among the state colleges in Maryland, the evening program at Morgan State holds a unique place. It is not being suddenly overrun by whites as is Bowie State, a former predominantly black state college near Washington, D. C. It is not isolated in the ghetto to almost exclude the whites as is Coppin State, in inner-city Baltimore. It seems, therefore, that some necessary steps should be taken to attract white students who are apparently hesitant while anxious to attend. The following steps have been initiated:

1. resolving small racial conflicts between and among black and white teachers and students as they have occurred;

2. cooperating with the coordinator of integration by asking him to counsel white evening students who have the need to talk out a problem, or suggesting white evening students who could help develop his program;

3. seeing that white students work with black students on the common problems of evening students;

4. hiring a part-time white counselor who, as does the black counselor, works with all students;

5. developing an extension program at the Social Security Center for Continuing Education;

6. Reminding white students to invite friends to noncredit courses, such as an income tax seminar and to cultural events at the college.

Development of this program with measurable gains is not yet accomplished, but the insistence that whites who wish may attend Morgan State College continues to gain support.

Drop-outs, Young and Old

Working with the white student as counselor or teacher in the black college is an exercise in helping him to see the traumatic experience of current changes and conflicts--and he may need referral--against whatever goals he may have for the future. He may have dropped out of high school, out of college, and probably out of the urban center city to move to a suburb as an escape from the encroaching black community. Often the outer rim of the city or the suburbs has placed him near the black college which was previously isolated from the central city. Often the black college, unable to move in urban planning, may become visible from new through-streets or from a new expressway, to the suburbs. The white student often says that "he just happened by." He reveals that he must get a degree in his present field or in a new one. He needs the degree in order to understand the economic structure and control his community services by his vote; in order to have a satisfactory social or recreational life for or within his family or by himself if he is alienated from his family.

What is the age of the white student? There are certain to be only a few teenagers, 17 or 18 years of age, as most of these would seek a four-year college out-of-town or one of the available community colleges. The observable pattern of busing white high school students of a changing neighborhood to public or private high schools elsewhere is a habit not easily broken. White teenagers, accustomed to busing, would hardly take a public bus or the family car or even their own motorcycles to ride to a black college, especially if a less expensive community college or a predominantly white four-year college or an urban branch of a large university exists in the same metropolitan area.

Hardly a black college today does not have such competition. Left to attend the predominantly black college is the young white student whose family may not have left a changing neighborhood, who, if male, is anxious to avoid the draft (and his father may appear at the black college with him) who, if male or female, may be just "turned off" by the whole idea of escape to the suburbs and finds his own apartment in order to remain in his old neighborhood. He or she then drifts over to the black college. There is also the young white student who has been developing his own ideas in his highly-integrated high school and becomes curious about the black college or sees its relevancy to his ideas about the city.

On the other end of the age range is the senior citizen, 70 years or over, who would not be expected to attend a predominantly black college. Those in the immediate neighbor-

hood are hesitant and fearful about leaving their homes for
any reason. They are immersed in old prejudices about the
quality of learning and facilities of the black school and the
attitudes of blacks toward them. Courses for cultural enrichment which they might select may seem to be heavily weighted
with alien cultural references and a utilitarian purpose in
which they are not interested.

There is also a group of whites approaching retirement, 59 to 69 years of age, who are less likely to attend a
predominantly black college because of feelings of security in
their employment or protection of status in the community.

The greatest focus must be on the white student 19 to
58 years old, divided into four classifications: the young
adult 19 to 28; the older young adult, 29 to 38; the young
middle-aged adult, 39-48; and the middle-aged, 49 to 58
years old. It should be noted that these classifications, while
arbitrary, are related to the writer's experience. Further
study of their problems based on an interpretation of the current U. S. census reports would reveal amazing insights into
cultural and other changes. The white student in these age
ranges may indicate that after he has dropped out of the fast-
changing city or while he is trying to exist within it, he is
willing to use any means to achieve both materialistic ends
and his identity even if he must involuntarily resort to, or
voluntarily chooses to attend, a predominantly black college.

Often he arrives at the college rather furtively, whether he be young or older, by himself or with a similarly anxious white potential student or protective ally, and hopes that
none of his white associates will wonder why he is there, perhaps even voicing this anxiety. He may say carelessly that
he doesn't care, or it doesn't matter where he gets a college
education or who teaches him. What background does he bring
to this anticipated learning experience in the black college?

The young white sutdent 19-28 years old has found a
job immediately after high school. He may have acquired it
during the work and study experience of high school. He
may, instead, have had his experience as a draftee in the
armed services. He may have had an unsuccessful experience in another college and now wishes to complete his college education without losing too many credits.

The older young adult, has still retained the semblance
of youth and immaturity. Without a college education, he re-

veals that he is insecure when the young college-trained white
or black comes on his job. He speaks sadly and/or jealous-
ly of not being able to take advantage of an earlier opportunity to go to college. In business or industry, he moves with
automation and has had several on-the-job training courses
but believes them to be no real substitute for the status he
feels a college degree would give.

The young middle-aged adult, 39 to 48 years old, may
be a serviceman returning from 20 years in the armed services who has decided on teaching, social work or law enforcement. This person may be a female teacher who has been
secure in 15 to 20 years of teaching begun at the time school
desegregation was being debated and resisted and housewives
were eased into the breach made by teachers leaving abruptly for other locations. The male teacher in this age group
may have had years of training in carpentry or plumbing and,
happening to fall into teaching, has remained there undisturbed
until qualifications and up-dating of training were declared essential.

Finally, the older middle-aged white potential student,
49 to 48, too young to accept retirement but perhaps in the
last years of a supervisory or administrative position, is attracted to the black college through what he feels is pressure
from those who are his responsibility to advise in business,
industry, teaching, law enforcement, or the social agency.
He may speak of cultural improvement, but he may also reveal that he wants to be brought up-to-date with information
to ease his underlying worry of competition from his associates. Each of the persons in these age groups reveals a
sense of urgency for college training and expresses great
disappointment, as in the instance of those seeking vocational education in a liberal arts college, if the predominantly
black college has been the last resort.

The concern of the counselor, faculty member or administrator in the predominantly black college, however, is
in assisting the white student to be involved with the changes
of the future rather than with the barriers of the present.
Immersed in the traditional fears of economic or on-the-job
competition, religious differences, or his national background
(and I have not discussed the significant problem of the white
middle-eastern immigrant in the black college), the white student certainly needs guidance for the technological society of
the future. However, on the black campus with race less of
a distinct barrier, he must be directed to the human relation-

ships which lie ahead. The black or white counselor, himself entrenched in traditions, must best learn how to assist
this white student, already disoriented in the black educational setting, and to prepare him for a world technological in
living and working experience but humanistic in person-to-
person relationships, eliminating old differences and prejudices.
Presented here are several guidelines for counseling the white
student in the predominantly black college:

1. helping the white student to develop his own goals
    of expected satisfactions in a college which has
    the added dimension of adjustment to the differing
    roles of minority on-campus and majority off-
    campus, the minority on-campus being white stu-
    dents;

2. helping the white student to recognize common
    yet individual problems of choice of major, finan-
    cial need, family or job conflicts with the college
    experience on the black campus where the pres-
    sures for survival are greater;

3. establishing the white student's confidence and
    ease in visiting or telephoning the college and
    becoming acquainted with services in addition
    to those of the counseling centers;

4. presenting with adequate publicity the inclusive
    racial policy of the black college; the special pro-
    grams of different emphases from those of pre-
    dominantly white colleges and the extensive coun-
    seling services open to all students; and

5. presenting additional contact by calls or letters
    to the white student's supervisor, employer, or
    social worker inviting them to be supportive ad-
    visors or perhaps adjunct faculty in this new col-
    lege experience (new ways of support to the white
    student completely alienated from family must
    also be devised).

[Future documentation of the problems of the white
student in the predominantly black college should be specific.]

Suggested References and/or Readings

Farmer, Martha L., ed. Student Personnel Services for
    Adults in Higher Education, Metuchen, N. J. Scarecrow
    Press, 1967.

Klein, Alexander, Natural Enemies: Youth and the Clash
    of 6f Generations, Philadelphia: Lippincott, 1969.

Knowles, Malcolm S., The Modern Practice of Adult Educa-
    tion, New York: Association Press, 1970.

Robinson, Armstead L., Foster, Craig C. and Ogilvie,
    Donald H., Black Studies in the University, New Haven,
    Conn.: Yale University Press, 1968.

Schwebel, Milton, Who Can Be Educated?, New York: Grove
    Press, 1969.

Slater, Philip, The Pursuit of Loneliness, Boston: Beacon
    Press, 1970.

Smith, Kerry G., ed., The Troubled Campus, San Francisco:
    Jossey-Bass, 1970.

Toffler, Alvin, Future Shock, New York: Random House,
    1970.

Young, Whitney M., Jr., Beyond Racism, New York: Mc-
    Graw-Hill, 1965.

Chapter XIII

COUNSELING INNER-CITY ADULTS
TO START HIGHER EDUCATION

by Hilda Hidalgo

This chapter will attempt to deal with the problem of
motivating inner-city adults to start higher education. The
views presented will be drawn mostly from personal experiences during my ten-year involvement with this problem in
the city of Newark, New Jersey. This experience has not
included significant work with Mexican-Americans, Oriental-
Americans, and other oppressed minorities and so I shall
not discuss them in this chapter.

The Inner City

In spite of shared characteristics, each inner city has
its own unique personality and it is not premature to state
that college counselors interested in serving the inner city
should study and understand the personality of their particular inner city.

The inner city is old. It claims seniority over its
neighboring suburbs. It achieved "city status" over contemporary neighboring municipalities that maintained "town status."

Suburbia and highways girdle the inner city. Into its
center, suburbanites are funneled into the morning traffic rush
and they are trickled out in the evening. During the working
hours the inner city hosts the rich, the powerful, the intellectual, the upward-moving middle class. To many suburbanites the inner city is a necessary day-time nightmare
that makes possible their pleasant nights and weekend dreams.
The feeling of many suburbanites is that the inner city exists
for the convenience of the suburbs; it is a sort of a necessary nuisance.

For the most part, inner-city residents are a con-
glomerate of public housing tenants, welfare recipients,
under-employed, miseducated and discriminated-against
second-class citizens, slum dwellers, and senior citizens.

High density of people and low density of services are
the equation of the inner city.   Services are traditionally administered by institutions.   For multiple reasons (lack of
concern for the inner city resident seems to constantly be
at the top of the list) institutions have not served the inner-
city residents.   It is common for the inner-city resident to
view institutions with hostility and distrust.

The community spirit is found in very small geographical areas--a block, a floor of a building, one tenement--
rather than in large areas such as school districts, political
districts, and the like.   At times the community spirit is
divorced from a geographical area.   It is found in churches,
ethnic clubs or organizations.   Often the community spirit
is killed or not allowed to flourish by the harsh demands of
the daily struggle for survival.

The inner city is polluted, abundant in old and new
slums, torn by the urban renewal bulldozer, bankrupt by a
dwindling tax base, burning with racial conflict, ridden with
crimes ... and so the litany of negation could continue.

For all its misery, the inner city is abundant in potential.   It is essential to the survival and well-being of
America.   The inner city still holds the nerve center of industry and it still houses great institutions of higher education.   It remains as a center of cultural enrichment.   Perhaps of greatest importance, the inner city holds the greatest
challenge and opportunity for America.   The challenge is to
stop and then reverse the trend of human deterioration so
evident in the inner city lest, like the drug problem, it
sprawls outward to the whole country.   The opportunity is
to free the unused talent, the natural resources present in
the inner-city resident.

Profiles of Inner-City Residents

In attempting to present inner-city resident profiles,
we recognize the danger of stereotyping.   In spite of this
danger, we believe that there is validity in drawing pictures
that represent recognizable clusters of inner-city residents
that we have come to know.   The pictures, due to their

very nature, leave out individual differences.

Blacks. The overriding consideration and characteristic of this group is Blackness. Being a Black in the American experience is a characteristic that transcends any individual trait that the members of this group might or might
not have. Blackness translates itself into: being abused;
being the victim of violence; lacking opportunity; knowing
more than what should be one individual's share of hate;
mistrusting as a reflex; and never daring to hope. The talk
of significant change in the realities of a Black man's life
are more myth than fact. Although it is better disguised today, the emphasis is still to make Blacks white as a pre-
condition to acceptance. The Black man knows intuitively
what the researcher must utilize all the tools of his science
to find out: that the rate of unemployment of young Black
men is the same among high school graduates and nongradu-
ates. To the Blacks, "Black Power" is a goal to achieve
rather than a present reality. To most Blacks, the institutions of higher education are either highest in the hierarchy
of schools which force their "dropping out" and/or powerful
wheels in the urban renewal bulldozer which evicts them.

Puerto Ricans. Color them poor with a hue of blackness. The Puerto Ricans are denied the right to be what
they are, Puerto Ricans. Different from Whites and Blacks,
they are constantly forced to identify themselves in the very
same American racist terms. If he resists, the Puerto
Rican finds himself in conflict and rejected by both Black
and White. Abuse, victimization, violence, lack of opportunity, distrust, hopelessness and self-hate, repeat themselves as a ditto copy of the Black reality. In cities where
Puerto Ricans and Blacks share the misery, the Puerto Ricans are still lower on the totem pole.

Often Puerto Ricans are de-personalized by lumping
them in compartments labled "Spanish-speaking" or "Black"
or "Latins". This labeling occurs frequently when program-
matic interventions, fantasized to meet the needs of the
Puerto Ricans as an annex to other group needs, are inven-
ted. The results have been that when this approach is used,
the other groups are served and the Puerto Ricans are not.

The most evident and constant characteristic of the
Puerto Rican is his reluctance to commit cultural suicide
or yield to cultural genocide.

Inner-City Whites.   Often the white left in the inner
city are the "enforcement troops" of other white racism.
They are trained to believe that their shaky financial position is the result of Black inadequacies or Black Power
cries that command preferential treatment of Blacks at the
inner city white's expense.   Their Black paranoia is re-
enforced by their physical proximity to nonwhites.   Their
escape to the suburbs has been prevented by life circumstances.   Their status is therefore dependent on how successful they are in retaining power and control over nonwhites.
They have been alienated by liberal White America, whom
they hate and distrust with the same passion with which they
hate and distrust Blacks.   Their educational level is often
below high school and seldom does it go beyond a high school
diploma.   This group views institutions of higher education
with distrust, hate or indifference.

These whites live in lower-middle and middle-class
ghettos.   They have a virtual monopoly of white- and blue-
collar positions.   Through unions and associations, they successfully enforce the "no Blacks-no Puerto Ricans" policy.
They are looked upon as a powerful political force even in
cities where they are numerically outnumbered by nonwhites.

Senior Citizens.   Many recipients of social security checks
depend exclusively or predominantly on these benefits.   Such
social security dependents often constitute another kind of inner city resident.   Predominant realities in their lives are
fear and loneliness.   Closeted and isolated, they seem to
mark time just waiting for the end.   If White, they live in
integrated public housing units, or in deteriorating housing
adjacent to the Black ghetto.   If Black, they usually live in
the worst housing in the ghetto.   Although motivating this
group of senior citizens to start college seems to be impracti-
cal from many points of references, the universities must try
to be relevant to these groups also in their adult education
nondegree programs.

Main Characteristics of Higher Education in Relation
to the Needs of Inner-City Adults

There is a consensus that higher education needs to
change if it is to meet the needs of inner-city adults.   The
awareness of the need for change has brought about a great
deal of talk about change, but little significant action.   In
fact, the most prevalent characteristic of higher education
is its resistance to change.   The prevailing view in higher

education circles is still that which was voiced by S. I.
Hayakawa: "Higher education is a sanctuary for debate and
scholarship uninterrupted by secular problems. " A study of
university and college faculty attitudes by David Borland reported that desire for faculty satisfaction is predominant in
our institutions of higher education. Faculty satisfaction
with the status quo acts as a deterrent to change.

Grade credits, standard and nonstandard tests, required courses, and prerequisites are still the everyday
practice of higher education, be it at the university or community college. These practices provide a solid fence designed to keep the inner-city resident out.

Higher education in America has historically been a
continuation of the "melting pot. " To the institutions of
higher education, immigrants in the past have gone to a-
chieve "final integration. " A large portion of inner-city
residents are rejecting the melting pot theory. These groups
are promoting a new form of integration based on cultural
plurality, an integration that reinforces cultural or ethnic
identity.

The student personnel-counseling profession is tied to
a tradition of passivity. Counselors are forced to wait in-
side office doors, during the office hours, for someone already motivated to come and ask for encouragement to do
what they have already decided they were going to do. The
concept of "aggressive casework" could be effectively borrowed by personnel workers. Succinctly, aggressive casework is a methodology of helping people who do not seek help
but could use it. The professional seeks out the potential
client, and "sells" his service. This approach comes in direct conflict with some "sacred practices" of the "helping"
professions. The acceptance of such an approach in college
personnel work will require a basic about-face in attitudes
and a change in ways of work. Unless this aggressive approach is adopted, however, the personnel officer might sit
forever in his isolated cubicle waiting for the opportunity to
motivate an inner-city adult to start higher education.

The National Association of Student Personnel Administration (NASPA) drew up some position papers for the attention and consideration of their membership. The ones
dealing with compensatory education, the student personnel
dean, and public relations are closely related to the problems of making higher education available to inner-city adults.

The intention of NASPA to make higher education a-
vailable to inner-city adults is evident. The difficulty is
that compensatory education (noncredit, remedial courses,
"general college" programs and other plans in which the
purpose is to compensate for imposed inadequacies in education) is unattractive to the inner-city adult. It labels him
"deficient. " Most programs of this sort require full-time
involvement, a luxury that inner-city residents cannot afford.

NASPA is clear and positive as to its intent to
achieve better communications between the university and all
segments of the community. The fact that NASPA sub-
mits the goal of better communication to all segments of the
community, as a position paper for membership consideration, implies, in my judgment, that such a goal represents
a departure from current practice. However, the statement
does not provide any enlightenment as to how this better
communication to all segments is to be achieved. I fear that
"the-better-communication-to-all-segments" goal will be adopted, but filed under the "no-action-except-in-crisis" category.
In a paper presented to the Adult Student Personnel Association, Inc. (ASPA), I suggested specific ways of improving
communication with the inner-city adult such as "the university establishing dialogues in factories and union halls; the
faculty making presentation to workers and writing nonjargon
articles to be published in union newspapers and similar publications. "[1]

Barring very few exceptions, free tuition and maintenance grants in significant amounts are not available for
inner-city adults. It is unrealistic to expect the inner-city
adults to use some of their hard-earned money (especially
in the first year) for tuition or other related expenses to
higher education. Unless "financial security" accompanies
the invitation to higher education, we are talking nonesense
as far as the inner-city adult is concerned.

Changes Designed to Make Higher Education Available
And Desirable to Inner-City Adults

In listing some of the main characteristics of higher
education and its relation to inner-city adults, some changes
have already been suggested which will make higher education available and desirable to them.

The time is past-due for the "talking" stages of change.
The implementation phase of change must begin. I am aware

of the difficulties or, at times, the impossibilities of expedit-
ing change.   However, I am suggesting that those people committed to change should best start acting forcefully about their
convictions or stop talking.   Change involves the acceptance
of risks: personal risks, collective risks, and institutional
risks.   The personnel worker that demands safety and guaranteed success to be built into his design of change is not serious about implementing change.   A first question each personnel worker must ask and answer himself is, "How committed
am I to change?" And then, "How committed to change is the
institution that employs me?"   In his answer to these two
questions, the worker will find the guiding principles to his
strategies of change.

Power is a pre-requisite in effecting change.   Personnel workers in colleges and universities often have very limited power, or do not recognize the power they do have.   My
first recommendation, therefore, is that personnel workers
examine the degree of power they do have and then go after
more.   To do this (in the context of our topic) personnel
workers must make alliances and coalitions with others that
share their perception of need to change the institutions they
serve in making them more accessible and desirable to the
inner-city adult.   Social-action-conscious students and mili-
tant-active inner-city adult groups are natural places to look
for support.

Inner-city residents reject the idea of seeking higher
education because both they and the college expect failure.
To be successful the counselor must begin to present to the
community concrete examples of success.   These successes
among the inner-city residents will be the best "recruiters"
and public relations officers the college will have in the inner city.   Success during the first year that an inner-city
resident attends college is crucial.   Some of the things a
counselor can do to help the inner-city resident achieve success during his first year are to insure that the student is free
of anxieties related to finances, (is financial assistance provided? are the payments held up by bureaucratic red tape
or inefficiency? was the assessment of the student financial
needs a realistically accurate one?)   Since most inner-city
residents have not had the opportunity to budget in long-term
blocks, monthly grants are better than semester or year
grants; and insure academic success.   There is evidence
to support the statement that a failure in one course during
the first year of college for the inner-city resident is often
the one reason for the student's dropping out of college.   Our

experience strongly suggests that the difference between success and failure, learning and not learning (especially for the
inner-city resident) is directly related to who is teaching a
specific course.   Therefore, the counselor must know the instructors and courses that optimize the opportunity of success
for the inner-city resident and he should share this information with the student.   This suggestion lends itself to "sticky
problems":   ethical considerations related to the counselors'
judgment, and his sharing such judgment with students, or
the competency of individual instructors and the relevancy of
specific courses.

Earlier it was stated that blackness is the overriding
characteristic of Black students.   Also it was stated that the
most evident and constant characteristic of the Puerto Rican is
his reluctance to yield to cultural genocide.   However, the curricula of most institutions are white and consequently are rejected by many nonwhite inner-city residents.   Black studies
and ethnic studies could well be used as the content of compensatory education programs having two values, that of legitimate
areas of study and as helpers in promoting group identity and
pride.

Compensatory education is often the open door for
admittance of inner-city adults to college.   Compensatory
education as it is presently and predominantly administered,
is bound to fail both as a means of encouraging adults to
enter college and as a way of preparing them to succeed in
college.   The noncredit status of such programs is viewed
by inner-city adults as a waste of time or as an investment
leading nowhere.   In terms of the "now" orientation that
characterizes the inner-city adult, such programs are unde-
sirable.   In addition, compensatory programs are often administered by the same people who originally failed to teach
and motivate those persons in the past.   It is no wonder that
the "expectancy of failure" is so prevalent in the minds of
both teachers and students.

In motivating inner-city adults to start higher education, there are few, if any, experts.   It is mostly virgin
territory into which the counselor must venture without the
benefit of tried blueprints of success.   The counselor must,
therefore, approach the challenge with a willingness and an
attitude of learning from his target population as to how he
can best serve them.   He must be persistent in his invitation without pushiness and hostility.   He has the dual responsibility of motivating the inner-city adult to enter college,

and motivating the college to serve the inner-city adult. The challenge is a difficult must.

Reference

1. Hildalgo, Hilda A. "The Merging of the Isolates", Learning to Change - A Social Imperative, A. S. P. A. Convention Proceedings, December 1969, Washington, D. C. pp. 13-22.

Suggested Further Readings

Browne, Robert S. , "The Challenge of the Black Student, " Freedomways, Fall 1968.

Campbell, Alan D. , ed. , The States and The Urban Crisis, Englewood Cliffs, N. J. : Prentice-Hall, 1970.

Chamberlain, Philips, "Obstacles to Change in the University", N. A. S. P. A. Journal, Vol. 8, no. 1, July 1970.

Cordoso, Jack J. , "Ghetto Blacks and College Policy", Liberal Education, October 1969.

Dorsett, Lyle W. , The Challenge of the City 1860-190, Lexington, Mass. : D. C. Heath, 1968.

Educational Policies Commission, Univeral Opportunity for Education Beyond High School, Washington, D. C. : National Education Association, 1964.

Furness, W. Tood, "Racial Minorities and Curriculum Change, " Educational Record, Fall 1969.

Gordon, Edmund W. and Wilkerson, Doxey A. , Compensatory Education for the Disadvantaged, New York: College Entrance Examination Board, 1966.

Kauffman, Joseph F. , "New Challengers to Student Personnel Work, " N. A. S. P. A. Journal, Vol. 7, no. 1, July 1970.

Lowe, Jeanne R. , Cities in a Race With Time, New York: Random House, 1967.

McConnell, T. R., "Student Personnel Services: Central or Peripheral?" N. A. S. P. A. Journal Vol. 7, no. 1, July 1970.

Robinson, A. L., et al., Black Studies in the University, New Haven, Conn.: Yale University Press, 1969.

Truman, David B., "The Academic Community in Transition: Visible Continuities and Invisible Changes,", N. A. S. P. A. Journal, Vol, 8, no. 1, July 1970.

Wilcox, Preston R., "It is Not a Replica of the White Agenda," in the Panel, "The Black Agenda for Higher Education," College Board Review, Spring 1969.

Wisdom, P. E. and Shaw, K. A., "Black Challenge to Higher Education," Educational Record, Fall 1969.

Woodring, Paul, "The Coming of the Common College," Saturday Review, June 21, 1969.

INDEX

A

ADULT
Age, 32-33
Definition of, 32
Effect of mobility on, 35
Psychological maturity, 33-34
Social role, 34-35
ADULT BEHAVIOR
Mobility and, 35
Need of counselor to understand, 132-133
Psychology of, 33-34
ADULT COUNSELING, see also
COUNSELING
Availability of, 21
Categories of, 22-29
Continuing Education and, 29
Definition of, 21-22
is Different, 32-37
Forms of, 35
Future needs, xii
and Group Therapy, 36
Implications for of differences
from youth, 18-20
Need demonstrated by Brooklyn
College, xi
Need for psycho-social basis,
35
Reactions to, 35
Scope of, 20-29
ADULT EXPERIENCES
Evaluated by Brooklyn College,
xi
Evaluated by the College Entrance Examination Board, xi
Need to recognize, xii, 19
Support for evaluation, 33
ADULT HIGHER EDUCATION
in England, x
History of, ix-xi
Impact of GI Bill on, x-xi
in Massachusetts, x
in Scandinavia, x

ADULT LEARNING YEARS, 33
ADULT, MINORITY GROUP
Counselors for, 136-138
Definition of, 134
Life style of, 135-136
Recommendations for counseling, 141
Techniques of counseling, 138-140
ADULT PSYCHOLOGY
and Age, 34
ADULT STUDENT
Definition of, 32
Differences from youth, 18-20
Educational interests of the, 19
Effect of mobility on the, 35
and Expectations from vocational counseling, 66-70
and Expectations from vocational counselor, 67-69
Goals of the, 19
and the Graduate Student, 94
Motivation of the, 19-20
Nature of the, 18
ADULT STUDENT PERSONNEL
ASSOCIATION, v
ADULT WOMEN
Concerns of, 27
Continuing education for, 27
Counseling, 26-28
and Vocational counseling,
69-70
ADVISING
and counseling, 40-41
AGE, 32-33
and Adult psychology, 34
and Social Role, 34
AKRON, UNIVERSITY OF
Testing and Counseling Bureau, 42
ALPHA SIGMA LAMBDA
Financial Aid, 105

167

168

of, 87
and Observation, 84-85
Orientation as a setting for, 81
Paraprofessionals, training and
  use of in, 87
Planning important in, 85
Referrals, 86
Registration as a setting for,
  81
Role of faculty in, 87
Techniques of, 84-85
Training in the methodology of,
  86-87
Use of case histories in, 87
COUNSELOR OF ADULTS, see
  also VOCATIONAL COUNSELOR
Adult perceptions of the, 80
and Adult psychology, 36-37
Availability of the, 29, 83
Important tasks of the, 19
of Inner City adults, 160
for Minority group adults,
  136-138
Need for sensitivity, 46, 84
Need to be alert, 82-83
Professional limitations of
  the, 47
Role of the vocational, 64-66
and Short term counseling, 81
Training of, conference on, 21
Training in the methodology of
  short term counseling, 86-87
CREDIT CARDS
Use of as financial aid, 106
CULTURALLY DEPRIVED
Counseling the, 29

Counseling adults with, 39-59
Counseling for, 49-50
Improper orientation, 44-45
Inadequate study skills, 43
Irrelevancy and conflict, 44
Lack of confidence, 43
the Learning and Study Skills
  Center and, 53-55
Meaning of, 39
Poor educational background,
  42-43
and other Psychological prob-
  lems, 45-47
Significance in higher education,
  39
Types of, 42-45
Unrealistic expectations, 43-
  44
EMPLOYMENT SECURITY, 28
ENGLAND
Adult higher education in, x
EXTRA-CURRICULAR ACTIVI-
  TIES
Counseling adults through,
  128-133

for Law enforcement officers,
103
Model Cities and, 104
National Defense Student Loans,
104
New Careers, 104
for the Retired Adult, 106
Scholarship funds, 105
Social Security Benefits, 103
Tuition postponement, 105
United States Association of
Evening Students, 106
use of Credit Cards as, 106
for Veterans, 102-103
Work Study as, 106-107
FORD FOUNDATION
and tuition postponement, 105
FOREIGN STUDENTS
in graduate schools, 93
financial aid for, 102
FRINGE BENEFITS
and financial aid, 107-108

G

GARCIA, PHILIP L., vi
GARDNER, JOHN, 25
GI BILL
Impact on Adult Higher Educa-
tion, x-xi
GRADUATE STUDENT
and the Adult student, 94
Bureaucracy and the, 92-93,
95
Counseling the, 89-96
Counseling needs of the, 89-
90
Counseling problems of the,
89
and Financial Aid, 101-102
the foreign, 93
Housing problems of the, 91-
92, 95
Placement of the, 93-94
GROUP
Activities as a setting for
counseling, 128-133
Counseling, 50-51
Counseling of minority group
adults, 139
Orientation as a setting for
short-term group counseling,
81

Therapy and adult counseling,
36

H

HIRD, PHYLLIS Y., v
HOUSING
Problems of the graduate stu-
dent, 91-92

I

INNER CITY
Description of, 156-157
Profiles of residents, 157-159
INNER CITY ADULTS
Counseling the, 156, 165
Making higher education a-
vailable and desirable to,
161-164
INNER CITY WHITES
Profile of, 159
IOWA EMPLOYMENT SECURITY
COMMISSION, 28

K

KABACK, GOLDIE RUTH, 22
KENDALL, RALPH, ix
KNOWLES, MALCOLM, 16, 18,
30

L

LAW ENFORCEMENT OFFICERS
Financial aid for, 103
LEARNING AND STUDY SKILLS
CENTER, 53-55

MC

MCCLUSKY, HOWARD, 33

M

MASSACHUSETTS
Adult Higher Education in, x
MATURITY, see PSYCHOLOGICAL
MATURITY
MOBILITY
Effect of on adults, 35
MODEL CITIES, 28
and Financial aid, 104

MONDALE, SEN. WALTER F.,
25
MORGAN STATE COLLEGE,
143-178

N

NATIONAL ASSOCIATION OF
STUDENT PERSONNEL AD-
MINISTRATORS, 160-161
NATIONAL DEFENSE STUDENT
LOANS, 104
NEW CAREERS, 28
and Financial aid, 104

O

OCCUPATIONAL UPGRADING
PROGRAMS, 28
OHIO STATE UNIVERSITY
COUNSELING CENTER, 42
ORIENTATION, 44-45
as a setting for short-term
counseling, 81

P

PARAPROFESSIONALS
Counseling of, 28-29
as Facilitators of counseling
for adults, 87
Training and use of in short-
term counseling, 87
PLACEMENT
of the graduate student, 93-94
PSYCHOLOGICAL MATURITY,
33-34
Difficulty in measuring, 33
PUBLIC SERVICE CAREERS, 28
PUERTO RICANS
Profile of inner city, 158

R

REFERRALS
Faculty's knowledge and use
of, 87
As a goal of short-term counsel-
ing, 86
The problem of, 47-49
and Testing, 48-49
RETIRED ADULT STUDENTS
Counseling, 24-26

Financial aid for, 106
Motivation, 24-25
Planning for, 34
Reduced tuition for, 26
RETIREMENT OPPORTUNITY
PLANNING CENTER, 25-26
see also DRAKE UNIVER-
SITY

S

SCANDINAVIA
Adult Higher Education in, x
SCHOLARSHIP FUNDS, 105
SENIOR CITIZENS
Profile of in inner city, 159
SHORT-TERM COUNSELING,
see COUNSELING, SHORT-
TERM
SOCIAL ROLE, 34-35
and age, 34
SOCIAL SECURITY
and Financial aid, 103
recipients of in inner city,
159
SOCIALLY DISADVANTAGED
Counseling the, 29
STUDY SKILLS, 43

T

TESTING
Referrals for, 48-49
in Vocational counseling, 61,
63
THOMPSON, CLARENCE H., v
TUITION
reduced for retired adults, 26
TUITION POSTPONEMENT, see
also FINANCIAL AID
Ford Foundation and, 105
at Yale University, 105

U

UNITED STATES ASSOCIATION
OF EVENING STUDENTS, 106

V

VETERANS
Educational needs, x
Financial aid for, 102-103